Playing a
New Game

T0371795

Playing a New Game

A BLACK WOMAN'S GUIDE TO BEING WELL AND THRIVING IN THE WORKPLACE

TAMMY LEWIS WILBORN, PhD

balance

NEW YORK BOSTON

Balance
Hachette Book Group
1290 Avenue of the Americas, New York, NY 10104
grandcentralpublishing.com
@grandcentralpub

Originally published in hardcover and ebook by Grand Central Publishing in October 2022.
First Trade Edition: March 2025

Balance is an imprint of Grand Central Publishing. The Balance name and logo are trademarks of Hachette Book Group, Inc.

The publisher is not responsible for websites (or their content) that are not owned by the publisher.

The Hachette Speakers Bureau provides a wide range of authors for speaking events. To find out more, go to hachettespeakersbureau.com or email HachetteSpeakers@hbgusa.com.

Balance books may be purchased in bulk for business, educational, or promotional use. For information, please contact your local bookseller or the Hachette Book Group Special Markets Department at special.markets@hbgusa.com.

Library of Congress Cataloging-in-Publication Data
Names: Wilborn, Tammy L., author.
Title: Playing a new game : a Black woman's guide to being well and thriving in the workplace / Tammy L. Wilborn, PhD.
Description: First edition. | New York : Balance, 2022. | Includes index.
Identifiers: LCCN 2022019459 | ISBN 9781538708347 (hardcover) | ISBN 9781538708361 (ebook)
Subjects: LCSH: Minority women in the professions. | Minority women—Employment. | Minority women—Psychology. | Minority women—Health and hygiene.
Classification: LCC HD6057 .W55 2022 | DDC 331.408—dc23/eng/20220511
LC record available at https://lccn.loc.gov/2022019459

ISBNs: 9781538708354 (trade pbk.), 9781538708361 (ebook)

Printed in the United States of America

LSC-C

Printing 1, 2024

This book is dedicated to my late grandmother,
Alma Marie Jordan,
and my mother, Alma Marie Rosemond.
Your struggles and sacrifices were not in vain.
I pray that you are proud.

CONTENTS

Playing a New Game

Introduction

I wish I didn't have to write this book. I wish that all the recent hype about #BlackGirlMagic matched the reality of Black women's lives. Arguably, Black women are winning right now! In 2020, Kamala Harris became the first Black woman to be elected vice president of the United States. Former first lady Michelle Obama took over the literary world with her *New York Times* best-selling book *Becoming*. Queen Beyoncé is still the queen! Black women are making a significant impact in every major industry, and closer to home, in my hometown of New Orleans, Black women are making history. In 2018, New Orleans elected LaToya Cantrell as its first Black woman mayor. A New Orleans native, chief justice Bernette Joshua Johnson was the first Black woman (and Black person) elected to the chief position in the Louisiana Supreme Court. Sevetri Wilson, entrepreneur and tech start-up founder, is the first Black woman in Louisiana to raise over $1 million in venture capital. Then there's Raynell "Supa Cent" Steward, founder of the multimillion-dollar makeup brand Crayon Case. Without a doubt, Black women are shining!

We are cultural influencers who are leading the dialogue on everything from beauty to politics. We are leading social movements that bring awareness, advocacy, and action to the issues that matter to us. We are, in essence, the shit! In the words of DJ Khaled, all we do is win, win, win! #BlackGirlMagic, right? So why write a book about Black women's work? The answer is simple: We might be winning at work (kinda), but we ain't well at work.

Recently, I was invited to San Francisco by a group of Black and Latinx women in the tech industry to talk about my research and book project addressing Black women's work experiences. These women were leaders in tech, so I was quite grateful and honored to receive the invitation. When I arrived at dinner, I was immediately struck by the fact that these were young Black women in leadership positions for major tech companies. At their age, I was still in entry-level positions and wouldn't achieve what many of them managed to achieve professionally for many years to come. Except for one woman who I later learned was in her fifties, I was the second oldest woman at the table.

I also took note that every woman at the table had natural hair. As Black women, we know our hair is a situation—especially at work. Particularly in predominantly white work environments, your hair can be the subject of unwelcome conversation or gestures. ("Can I touch your hair?") Or worse yet, your hair can be the reason you don't get hired, promoted, or retained. So, the fact that these women were a group of BOSSES who were young, Black, gifted, AND natural in a white, male-dominated field like the tech sector got my whole entire life together!

Their energy and youthfulness were refreshing to observe. The table was buzzing with excitement as these women made new connections and reconnections. I enjoyed listening to them talk boldly and unapologetically about whatever the topic of the moment was, which was mostly some variation of the white folks at their jobs "doin' too much." When it seemed that their volume had reached a point that others outside of our table could hear them, I noticed my own reaction with some amusement: a mix of *Shhh, girl, they can hear you* and *Say it louder for the people in the back!* As I am a member of the cohort between the baby boomers and millennials, on any given day my own behavior usually falls somewhere on the continuum between respectful and revolutionary. Yet these younger women claimed their space unapologetically in a way that was refreshing to see.

When the host introduced me, I shared a little about my life story and my purpose in writing about Black women's work experiences before inviting the women to share their own experiences at work. My reasons for this invitation were twofold. On the one hand, as a professional counselor with twenty-plus years of experience (and about that much time as a client myself), I fully understand the therapeutic value of telling your story. For Black women in particular, it is imperative for us to have safe spaces where our experiences can be heard, validated, and normalized. My other reason was curiosity about their experiences as Black women leaders in industries dominated by white men.

At the outset, part of me wanted to believe I would hear something different from what I already knew from my research, clinical work, and experience. However, as they each shared their stories, the usual suspects emerged: feeling devalued, exploited, invisible, hypervisible, confused, frustrated, excluded, disrespected, and exhausted—things I'd heard many times before. Some of their stories highlighted the deleterious effects of chronic stressful work experiences. For example, one woman shared how the stress and pressure of work had led her to contemplate suicide only weeks prior to our conversation. Another woman shared how discriminatory treatment at work triggered her to take a leave of absence to seek inpatient mental health treatment. As I listened to these women one by one, my initial feelings of joy and excitement were replaced by sadness and anger. I saw myself in these young sisters. Like me, they had received the same messages: *"Get an education!" "Work twice as hard!" "Be grateful!" "Never let 'em see you sweat!"* And my personal favorite, *"You got to play the game!"*

I imagined them showing up like countless other young Black women early in their careers—bright eyed, eager, and ready to work (harder, that is). Their stories confirmed what I knew: Black women pay a tremendous cost when they internalize the well-intentioned yet harmful message that they need to do more if they want to get ahead at work. When unchecked, these messages lead to harmful stereotypes that hinder Black women's ability to seek help. If their stories are any indication, #BlackGirlMagic is a myth that, like all stereotypes, distorts the reality of Black women's lived experiences at work. When Black women work harder, we suffer. Sometimes, we die.

Work has been identified as a chronic stressor for Black women that affects our mental and physical health. According to the Centers for Disease Control and Prevention, heart disease is the leading cause of death for Black women of all ages and the second leading cause of death for Black women ages twenty-five to sixty-four.[1] Cancer is the second leading cause of death for Black women of all ages and the number one leading cause of death for Black women ages thirty-five to sixty-four, followed by stroke, diabetes, and chronic lower respiratory diseases (e.g., emphysema), which are the third, fourth, and fifth leading causes of death, respectively. Additionally, obesity is a health issue that significantly affects Black women. A 2018 report by the US Department of Health and Human Services' Office of Minority Health found that Black women have the highest rate of obesity compared to other groups in the United States and are 50 percent more likely to be obese than non-Hispanic white women.[2] Epidemiological studies show that heart disease, diabetes, and obesity have all been associated with adverse work experiences.[3] Relatedly, experiences of race and gender stereotypes at work have been associated with mental health issues such as depression, anxiety, addiction, and poor self-esteem—all of which can compound physical health issues.[4] Further, Black women have higher rates of depression compared to women of other racial and ethnic groups. Clearly, stress from work is not only making us sick but it is, in some cases, also killing us.

And yet, work stressors and their impact on wellness are absent from the current national discussion about Black women. Previous authors in the areas of career development and leadership not only have failed to address Black women's work experiences as a wellness issue but also have failed to discuss how race and gender stereotypes rooted in slavery and perpetuated by media create unique barriers that affect Black women personally and professionally. *Playing a New Game* begins to fill that void by highlighting that Black women's work experiences are a wellness issue that requires replacing antiquated and injurious messages with new messages that promote self-care and self-empowerment as necessary for any serious discussion about career advancement for Black women. If you've been seeking advice for managing your stress and maintaining your sanity at work, this book is for you. I will walk you through the harmful effects of stereotypes in the workplace and provide you with the tools to prioritize your mental and physical health. It's time to play a new game: one where you can be well *and* excel at work.

Chapter 1

"GET YOUR EDUCATION"

A wise man once said, "I will not live my life by any script other than the one I write." That man was my brother Tommy, who, like my sister Val, died at the age of fifty-five from heart disease. I happen to agree with Tommy. As a therapist, I've observed that much of the suffering and soul sickness that my clients often experience comes from unhealthy, unhelpful, and untrue messaging from their childhood that become the life scripts by which they perform poorly as adults. And as a therapist, I believe that part of my job is to help clients deconstruct these unhelpful messages and harmful behavior practices so that they can reconstruct a life script with messaging that allows them to be authentic, well, whole, and ultimately free. And for Black people, let me be clear: Freedom has always been our agenda.

The messaging I received about work came from two of the most important women in my life: my grammaw and my mama.

My experiences growing up with these two women were simultaneously the source of much strength and suffering in my own life and therefore the focus of many a future counseling session, if not most of them. Grammaw and Mama expected me to be everything they were not. Whether I wanted to be or not, I was the "hero" of the family. I was also the "smart" one; therefore, my success was the family's success.

Nobody told me that in so many words. They didn't have to. It was felt. From a family counseling perspective, everyone plays a role in their family. These roles are reciprocal and reinforcing and, no matter how dysfunctional, are intended to maintain the balance of the family structure. Step outside of your role, and your family will be sure to let you know you're out of line and to get back in it...fast! I've counseled many clients who were trying to break free of family roles that no longer served them, if they ever did. In my family, my role as the hero and the smart one gave my mama and grammaw bragging rights, if to no one other than themselves, that they had done something right and perhaps that their sacrifices were not in vain. But for all its advantages, my script as the hero and smart one came with a cost—the full price of which I would not know until many years later.

My grammaw died in February 2018 at the age of ninety-seven. As the matriarch of our family, she was a survivor and pillar of faith, strength, wisdom, and fight. And yet, my grammaw was a complicated woman with an even more complicated history and story. To me, she was everything a grandmother should be: wise, encouraging, nurturing, kind, and loving. Some of my fondest memories of her were moments between the two of us, which were rare after the birth of my two younger sisters. We had a special relationship—I knew I was her favorite and so did everyone else, although in my adulthood, knowing this has brought more frustration than joy. My grammaw had a host of grandchildren and great-grandchildren who needed and wanted everything I received from her as her favorite but did not get, a fact that I could neither celebrate nor change.

As a kid, I spent lots of time with Grammaw mostly because my mother was a single divorced woman who needed someone to watch me and my sisters when she needed to work. Or go out. Or keep her sanity. Or a combination of all those things, especially as a young woman and mother. Sometimes these visits lasted a few days—over a weekend usually. At times these "visits" lasted for months, especially during the summer when my grammaw would show up in her silver Dodge Caravan, sometimes unannounced, to haul me and my sisters off to Tylertown, Mississippi, for a summer of misery. Tylertown most certainly had to be the town that Mayberry on *The Andy Griffith Show* was patterned after, except in Tylertown the police station was the size of a closet and...there were Black people.

Prior to Tylertown, I would visit Grammaw in New Orleans, where she lived in the Lafitte housing project. In second grade, I lived with Grammaw in the project for several months while my mother, who was pregnant with my sister Shannon at the time, lived with her boyfriend and his dad for reasons that were never really explained nor understood. The project was a far cry from Tylertown for several reasons, but primarily because, unlike Tylertown, there is never a dull moment in New Orleans. Ever. Even when nothing is going on, there is plenty going on and trouble to get into. And, certainly, way more Black folks! In the project, those two facts were not lost on Grammaw.

The Black folks in the projects in her mind were "niggas" who were not to be trusted and therefore not the kind of Black folks she wanted me, her favorite, to mix with. So, despite the fact that there was so much going on around me, there was nothing for me to do. She wouldn't let me play with the other children in the courtyard, which meant I usually ended up sitting on the porch with her throughout the day watching the cars go by, speaking to the "niggas" she liked (meaning the ones she deemed respectable in some way), and talking about the ones she didn't like.

The line between "nigga" and respectable was faint because respectability seemed, to me, to be based on some nebulous measure of decency. In other words, for Grammaw this meant those who worked or at least looked like they were heading to work, and the children who were clean and decent. If I was lucky enough (or rather if *they* were lucky enough), she would occasionally (meaning a handful of times) let them play with me on the porch under her watchful and scrutinizing eye. To Grammaw, I wasn't like those children. I was smart, clean, and important. And so it was, each morning with my neatly combed hair and pressed school uniform, a van picked me up to bring me to Catholic school.

The optics of the little girl from the projects being transported with private van service to her Catholic school were not lost on our neighbors. In New Orleans, the school you attend is a powerful social tool that city residents wield for influence, power, and respectability. After asking your name, the next most important question in a new social interaction is still, to this day, *What school did you go to?* As a Black woman, I hate this question now because I know it is a ridiculous social guidepost that gives the other person the opportunity to judge, like my grammaw would, what kind of "nigga" I am. But as a child living with Grammaw in the Lafitte, as far as I could tell, there was nothing different about the "niggas" who passed by out there and the ones who lived at 1702 Saint Peter Street, the address where we lived. Inside, we didn't live like we were better. I slept on a sofa that had a body-sized dent in it, mostly from my grammaw, whose bed it was the days I didn't sleep over. Anything of remote value or beauty at 1702 Saint Peter Street was either stolen by my uncle to buy drugs or destroyed when he couldn't get his drugs. If work was any measure of respectability and decency, by my account, my grammaw scrubbing white folks' toilets several times a month meant that the "niggas" out there were a reflection in the mirror she was trying hard not to see, and to convince me of the same.

The bus rides from the Lafitte to the white folks' houses my grammaw cleaned in the city and surrounding areas seemed like they took forever. I was always one to be curious and observant, and the long bus rides gave me plenty of opportunity to people watch as adults and kids hopped on and off at each stop, and gave my grammaw ample material to judge and joke about, which to my delight made the long rides worth all the hassle.

With every bus transfer, not only did the scenery change but so did the conversation. The closer we were to the white folks' houses, the cleaner and whiter the neighborhoods looked—a far cry from the grit and grime of the Lafitte. Seeing the white folks' neighborhoods must have been a cue for Grammaw, because she would say things to me that felt serious, that offered wisdom I needed to understand as if my life depended on it. Even when I was a young child, Grammaw had a way of talking to me like I had the understanding of grown folks; maybe she saw wisdom in my youth. Or maybe she assumed as the smart one, I'd get it. Being smart, she needed me to understand, was not only a gift from God but also a way out. A path to somewhere better. "Tammy, go to school and get your education!"—I understood that. I sensed that what she was doing was necessary, but it wasn't better. Grammaw had made her way to the big city of New Orleans to find work that was not picking cotton. Although she eventually earned a nursing aide certificate—which I learned was a proud moment for her because she had a respectable title—she felt that she could do better. Better was earning twenty dollars a day cooking and cleaning for white folks and caring for their children. This had its advantages. Some helped Grammaw with her own family, which ranged from providing mattresses for Mama and her siblings to assisting her with the purchase of a new car. In essence, then, better meant being a mammy. For me, not only did Grammaw want me to do better, but she also expected me to. She needed me to understand this. I did. The message of striving for better had been firmly planted. And it was a message that my mama would not only cultivate but also expand.

We are all born into the middle of someone else's story. In therapy, helping clients understand how others' stories fit into the mosaic of their own narratives can be a great source of clarity, meaning, and growth. Perspective is everything; how we think about and make meaning of our experiences influences how we feel and ultimately what we do. It is necessary if you are to live life authentically, well, whole, and free to deconstruct the stories you tell yourself about yourself and others to ensure that those messages are healthy, helpful, and true. As you reflect on your own story, ask yourself: What is the story that I tell myself about my own journey, and how has that story helped or hindered me along the way?

As you reflect on your own story, ask yourself: What is the story that I tell myself about my own journey, and how has that story helped or hindered me along the way?

WASH THEM TRAYS!

I entered my mother's story when she was a sixteen-year-old high school senior living with Grammaw and her older sister and two older brothers. By all accounts, life was hell. As you can imagine, twenty dollars a day was hardly enough to take care of a family of five even if you lived in the projects. It was a struggle to keep the lights on and take care of necessities. To make matters worse, remember the uncle who I told you became destructive when he couldn't get his drugs? Apparently, he was that way even as a kid; as my mother tells it, she spent many nights praying that either he would die or she would die, a thought that still saddens me to my core when I hear it. For Mama, her escape came in an unlikely form: pregnancy. For some teenagers, getting pregnant and not finishing high school would be the end of the road, but for Mama, it was the beginning of her own path to better.

In my early years, my mother and father lived together, and both worked in the service industry; Mama mostly bused tables or washed dishes, and Daddy worked as a cook. As an adult, I enjoy hearing the stories about these early work experiences because, like my grammaw, Mama has a wicked sense of humor, and so there's never a boring moment even if I've heard the stories a thousand times. However, over the course of my work as an adult, I realized that I didn't really know how my grandmother's work affected how my mama saw herself as a Black woman at work, and ultimately how that self-perception influenced how Mama navigated work and life. Talking with her has helped me to better understand not only her work story, but also how her story and the messages therein shaped my own. We often don't think about how our own work story fits into a larger family work story and the influence it has on our own. Take a minute to think about what you know about your mother's and grand-mothers' work stories. What connections do you notice between your story and theirs? How can better understanding their work story lead to a better understanding of your own?

Those conversations with Mama were fruitful for many reasons, particularly for bringing connection and clarity, which made the mosaic of our interconnected stories more beautiful. I felt an indescribable amount of humility and pride hearing my mother talk about the journeys that she and my grandmother traveled on to create better lives for their families. Even as I write this, I experience a surge of energy at the thought of what they endured so I could do the very thing I am doing right now: writing a book that will help Black women pack light on their own work journey. I was also shocked at my newfound respect for them.

It would be socially acceptable to say that I had an unconditional, unquestioned love and respect for Mama and Grammaw. But I didn't. Y'all know that in our culture, there is a sacred place that Black mothers hold. For some they can do no wrong, and saying anything bad about them is almost blasphemous. But Black mamas are human first. They are flawed. They can be toxic. They are not always positive. They are not always selfless. They are not superheroes. They are women who are also mothers. Truth be told, the mothers in my life had some shit with them. Some of their words and actions hurt me and others. They disappointed me; they caused me to feel shame and self-doubt. I loved them deeply as mothers, but I didn't always like them as women. That's my truth. It is what it is. But as I listened to my mother describe her journey, I was overcome by new respect and a bit of shame that I had ever judged her, and Grammaw, at all. These women were simply trying to write a new script. The real question is, what script will I write for myself now that the pen is in my hand?

The real question is, what script will I write for myself now that the pen is in my hand?

Like my grandmother, my mother stressed the importance of education. In third grade I was tested and was identified as a gifted student, so from that point forward Mama became very selective about the schools I attended to make sure they were academically rigorous, a selectivity I would maintain when it was time to choose college and graduate programs. Mama did not play when it came to my education and was a relentless advocate for me. When I failed the admissions test for a local magnet school in New Orleans, she called the school and somehow convinced the person responsible for admissions decisions that I "needed" to be in the school. I don't know what else she told the lady, but I know I was accepted and eventually graduated from high school there in 1994. As I recently learned, Mama's view of education as a vehicle to betterment wasn't just something she believed was true for me and my sisters. It was something she fiercely believed was true for her too. "God has been with me the whole entire time. You have to want more to do more… I've always wanted to finish college. I probably would have gone higher if I didn't have kids."

Mama shared with me a defining moment early in her work history, when she worked as a dishwasher at a nursing home. One day, her supervisor, a woman who immigrated from Jamaica, yelled out to her, "*Wash them trays!*" As I listened, Mama's voice grew louder, as it often does when she's irritated or angry (anger that even as a grown woman I try not to be on the receiving end of) as she recalled that moment: "It was something about the way she said that… '*Wash them trays!*' Here she was a woman from Jamaica who came over here to do better… for more opportunity… and I am from this country and I couldn't do better? She made me do better that day."

I tried to imagine what my mother must have felt in that moment, being treated like she was less than. I got mad! Not only at the thought of someone treating my mama that way, but also because I know that her experience is neither unique nor antiquated. It was not something that happened to Black women way back then. This type of foolishness still happens. Every. Single. Day. To Black women at work everywhere. And not just with white folks, although they are the main culprits, but also with people of color. Have you had a *wash them trays!* moment? That *not today* moment? That *do you know who I am?* moment? That *not today, Satan* moment? *Wash them trays!* was all those moments for Mama, but her story was about to change.

In 1979, at age twenty, Mama applied to and was accepted to the CETA program at the Dryades YMCA in New Orleans. In her words, "Girl, my ship came in when I got accepted into that program. That was my proud moment." She had learned from one of her girlfriends at the time that CETA, the Comprehensive Employment Training Act, was a government program signed into law by President Nixon to provide skills training and job placement for low-income individuals. For a teenage mother and high school dropout from the projects, CETA was the means to an uncertain but bright future—a path to better. From 1979 to 1980 she attended and completed the program, eventually earning her GED and a certificate of secretarial skills.

The day before Mama's welfare ended, she was hired for a job with the federal government, a job she worked from the time I was five until I turned thirty, eventually retiring with twenty-five years of service in 2006 after Hurricane Katrina. In full transparency, I never really knew what Mama did. Whenever someone asked, I would say, "Oh, my mama work for NASA," which wasn't exactly true. She actually worked for the United States Department of Agriculture, which was housed in the NASA building.

Tomatoes . . . *tomahtoes*!

In this case, Mama's *good* job had everything to do with the NASA facility itself. When I visited Mama at work over the years, I always felt a sense of pride at this massive facility, with its pristine shiny floors. There was a security checkpoint at the main entry; whenever Mama emerged from behind the security checkpoint, she seemed happy, that is until she got to me in the lobby, because with the exception of the annual Christmas party, my visits to her job usually meant I needed something—money, her car, something else.

Working for the federal government was a big deal, and it wasn't until my recent conversation with her that I learned that Mama was also a big deal: "Everybody knew me. They saw me as a beast...they cried when I retired!" Indeed, her government job was a long way from cooking and cleaning for white folks as Grammaw had done. And while different, it was clear that my grandmother's work experience heavily influenced how my mother viewed herself and ultimately how she navigated work. Respect was the name of the game.

My mama told me, "I definitely knew coming in [to work] that racism was real. I did not want to be treated like a nigger! I learned that from my mama, and she learned that from her mama. I saw her strength...she did not let white folks play with her. Mama did a lot of respectin' so she got respect!" It became evident to me that while I had an incomplete version of my mother's work experiences, it had always been clear that my mama did not tolerate disrespect. Of any kind. From anyone. Period. Like my grandmother, Mama was a fighter in every sense of the word: "I had to fight for my reputation. I was always willing to get fired for my rights!" Yup! That sounded about right. When I was growing up, she had taught me similar values, although back then she actually meant fighting the kids in the neighborhood if they messed with me. When the message is "fight them or I'm gonna whup your ass!" you learn quickly. It's not hard to guess which option I chose. And, although I never really developed the knack or skills for that kind of fighting—I lost more fistfights than I actually won—I never would have guessed years later that fighting for my rights, respect, and reputation would be the biggest fight of my life.

Think about your own family. I suspect you don't have to think hard about the implicit and explicit messages you've received as a Black woman about the need to fight.

The message to fight isn't unique to my own family. For Black families, being prepared and willing to fight to express the fullness of your humanity is a normal and necessary part of the socialization process. Think about your own family. I suspect you don't have to think hard about the implicit and explicit messages you've received as a Black woman about the need to fight.

I understood the fighting aspect of Mama's work story. However, there was another part of her story that was completely unknown to me. With the exception of hearing about my mother going back to college and graduating in her forties with her bachelor's degree in criminal justice, I felt cheated that I hadn't been told about her professional accomplishments during her twenty-five-year tenure with the federal government. There was the time in 1999 when she received a Congressional Medal of Excellence while working at the National Finance Center as a part of the team that successfully transitioned the payroll system for government agencies like the CIA and FBI to the new millennium. What in the entire——? Why didn't I know about this? A whole congressional medal and she ain't told nobody nothin? When I expressed this sentiment, she nonchalantly replied, "Girl, I don't know why you didn't know. That medal is somewhere in a box." Unbelievable.

Outside of the accomplishments, it also became clear that the narrative I had been telling myself about my mother's lack of career advancement was simply wrong. Here I had been telling myself (and even the audiences I spoke to) that my mother was overlooked for promotion when, in fact, not only had she been promoted, but there were also opportunities that she didn't pursue because she had a different agenda: "I was there for one reason: I had kids! I needed insurance. I was only passing by. I didn't want none of that shit... I was only supposed to be there five years." My mind was blown—all these years I had part of the story wrong.

I do not take complete responsibility for this. On the one hand, there were parts that were unknown because they simply weren't shared. On the other hand was the contrast of our home life. The reality was that Mama's good job never seemed to pay enough for us to live better or, at least, securely. Sure, our life was much different from the life she grew up in—but not by much. Similar to her own childhood, there were many times our electricity was cut off. Times when we had to rely on the help of others to pay our bills. We didn't live in the projects, but sometimes we definitely lived in the 'hood. The way we lived wasn't the worst, but it wasn't the best. Maybe it was good that I didn't know what was happening at work because it would have confused me more. But I always did know that my mother was doing what she thought was her best given her own background. Yet our lack of financial security always highlighted that she was falling short, a fact that undoubtedly caused her much guilt and shame.

AN EDUCATION

Fannie Lou Hamer once said, "There are some things I feel strong about...one is not to forget where I come from and the other is to praise the bridges that carried me over." It was because of God's grace; my mother and grandmother's prayers, persistence, and fight; and my own prayers and fight that I am here. I am clear about this. I am forever grateful to have a family that not only believed in education but also fought to ensure that I believed and understood its value as well. Outside of the birth of my children and my marriage, my academic accomplishments have been my proudest moments.

I wish I could say that my education has helped me to keep my lights on, pay all my bills on time, and not rely on others for financial help, but it hasn't. Getting my education hasn't necessarily led to any significant material gain. (Whenever you're ready to shower the blessings down, Lord, I'm ready to receive them!) That's a lie they sell us on. Go to school and get an education so you can live the American dream. For me, being educated means that I can walk upright, forward, and onward in power knowing where I came from and who and whose I am. I am a child of God. I am Alma's granddaughter and Alma and Tommy's daughter (my mother is named after my grandmother). I am a mother. A wife. And I am a doctor. I went from the 'hood to being hooded, so in the words of Cash Money CEO Birdman—put some respeck on my name!

Many people don't make it out of the 'hood because institutional racism is designed to keep its knee on Black people's necks. Some of us do. My mother's and grandmother's stories reflect a set of assumptions that getting an education will help you cross a bridge to somewhere better, which I have learned is neither necessarily true nor false. But for many of us, the belief or maybe hope that getting an education would make our lives better (and a belief in God) is all that Black folks had to give. It was all that my grandmother and mother had, and I am eternally grateful to them for their journey. As I continue to understand their path, my own path becomes clearer. All roads lead to where I am right now.

My story is your story. Your story is our story, and there is power in seeing your story reflected in someone else's. As you think about my story, what comes to mind about your own? What messages shaped your journey to where you are now? The goal is for you to be inspired and to encourage you to prioritize your well-being wherever your path takes you.

Chapter 2

"YOU'RE AN OVERACHIEVER"

I didn't always want to be a professional counselor. Like most, my career path is a winding road of random choices, short-lived interests, serendipity, and God's plan. As a kid, I wanted to be a fashion model, and at thirteen, I convinced my mother to send me to modeling school. I enjoyed every bit of the experience until we had to learn how to pose. Our instructors had us stand in front of a mirror and strike a pose based on the feelings they called out. "Look surprised!" I had seen Tyra Banks do this pose countless times in the magazines. However, posing on demand did not work for me. Tyra made it look easy—turns out it's the hardest thing ever. After several failed attempts to look surprised or whatever the emotion of the day was and a growing sense that modeling school was not in our household budget, my shot at being America's next top model was over.

In high school, I was sure that I was going to become a lawyer. In the fall of 1994, I enrolled at Loyola University New Orleans as a political science major. Sitting through political science classes was like listening to someone run their fingernails across a chalkboard. That and the fact that I would have to take the LSAT—and pass it—ruled out any chances of becoming the next Perry Mason. But then a thing happened! I took a psychology course, and it changed my life—and I changed my major. In 1999, I graduated from Loyola with a BA in psychology—and two months pregnant.

Jobs weren't exactly plentiful with a psychology degree. After a few months, I responded to a short ad for a position working with women and children, which turned out to be a shelter counselor position at a battered women's program. I wasn't exactly qualified; I had neither training nor credentials to provide mental health counseling. But I did have personal experience.

As a child, I witnessed my mother's abuse at the hands of her then husband and, later, a man she dated. I heard the screams in the middle of the night, broke up the fights, called the police, and missed days of school because of the domestic violence in my home. Therefore, I knew not only what it was like to grow up with domestic violence but also the impact of physical and emotional abuse on my mother. Not exactly the type of thing you discuss on a job interview, but I did. And it worked, because I got hired—although I was fired nine months later for inadvertently snitching on a co-worker's bad behavior; that co-worker happened to be my supervisor's cousin. In the streets they say snitches get stitches. At work, I guess snitches get pink slips.

Although I lost my job, I gained a new perspective. I realized that I not only enjoyed listening to and helping others, but I was also surprisingly good at it. And I could get paid doing it. I applied to and was accepted into the graduate counseling program at my alma mater, Loyola University New Orleans. The decision to attend graduate school was a good one—in 2003, I graduated with a 4.0 and a clear sense that counseling was my calling. The psychology degree paid off after all.

Think about the detours you've experienced along your own work journey. How did those experiences lead to where you are now? What lessons did you gain from those experiences to help you navigate your work journey?

READY TO SERVE

By fall 2003, with my master's degree and three-year-old son in tow, I headed to Memphis, Tennessee, to start a new life and build my career as a counselor for an agency that served children and their families. Despite my initial reservations about working with children, my own childhood experiences made it easier to understand the challenges these youths experienced. As a graduate student, I swore that I would never work with children. The messages I had internalized from my mother gave me the impression that children were bothersome, burdensome, and therefore bad. Working with children, then, was the last thing I wanted to do.

As luck or rather fate would have it, working with children was exactly what I ended up doing. However, clinical work with children gave me a different perspective. I learned that children are often the victims of circumstances that they have little control and agency over. Consequently, if children are not given a solid foundation to flourish, then they flounder. As a counselor, then, I was there to provide hope that with appropriate treatment and family support, a trajectory of success was possible. I took my professional obligation to show up for my clients very seriously—I was there to serve, not save. Their stories mattered. Their voices mattered. They mattered.

I took my professional obligation to show up for my clients very seriously—I was there to serve, not save. Their stories mattered. Their voices mattered. They mattered.

After four years, I became a licensed professional counselor and was promoted to a clinical leadership role; I was promoted again two years later to a senior clinical leadership role. These promotions were important professional milestones that reflected a hard-earned reputation as a solid clinician and advocate for the ethical and effective treatment and care of children and their families. However, my advocacy for clients was not always welcomed.

One day, a supervisor requested a meeting to discuss her concerns about a counselor who was her direct report, but under my clinical supervision. During the meeting, the supervisor showed a video of the counselor shoving a female resident into the wall. The supervisor looked at me and asked, "What should I do?" I said that the counselor needed to be terminated immediately, a point that I made clear to the director and eventually the chief clinical officer.

After some initial resistance from leadership, I decided that I would no longer supervise the counselor and would report her to the appropriate authorities if the company did not fire her and make the report. You might be saying yes, recommending the counselor be fired and refusing to work with her sounds like an appropriate course of action. Yet, as the only Black woman in that position at the time, it was a bold move to take a stand against the company for one child. A Black female child at that. The counselor was fired two days later. That experience was a defining moment of my career. I was standing on my professional ethics and sense of justice that doing the right thing is always the right thing to do.

While the counselor hitting a client was extreme, it represented a growing pattern that I noticed with the counselors in the program. The level of fragility and emotional instability displayed by some of the clinicians created significant barriers to their ability to provide effective client care, a fact that I was not shy in expressing to the counselors themselves or their supervisors. I became increasingly frustrated with the counselors' behavior and restless in my role. Within four years post-master's, I had accomplished all of my professional goals. I was licensed. I had been promoted several times. I was respected among my peers. Yet I knew something needed to change. So I decided to go back to school to get my doctorate in counseling at the University of North Carolina at Charlotte—with a new hubby and expanded family coming along.

THE "PERFORMANCE" REVIEW

In the beginning, things went well in Charlotte. I was able to transfer with my job and work part-time. While the atmosphere of the Charlotte office was quainter and family-like, I felt out of place. I was the new kid on the block; in Memphis, everyone knew me and my work. In Charlotte, I had a new supervisor, a new set of teams and program staff, and the uphill battle of the new folks learning and understanding my style and way of doing things. Further, dividing my time among home, work, and school meant little time for socializing with my new colleagues.

Early signs of danger came less than a year later. I was reprimanded by my supervisor for working from home for a few days because my baby was sick. In Memphis, the company culture was a family-friendly work environment. Most of my colleagues, including my supervisor, had young children, so bringing your child to work or needing to stay home to care for your sick child was a common practice.

Thus, I was legitimately confused when my supervisor suggested that we needed to meet to discuss these concerns. I questioned whether such a meeting was necessary. My supervisor, perhaps sensing that she was losing the battle, finally said, "Tammy, I am going to tell you like my boss told me: You made a choice to be a working mother. You may need to consider getting auxiliary childcare like a nanny or something if your child is sick." After rent, childcare expenses were the second largest expense we struggled to pay each week. The suggestion that we add a nanny to an already tight budget was not only absurd but also anxiety provoking. We couldn't afford the childcare we had. Where were we going to find money for this *auxiliary* childcare?

What hurt more was that my supervisor, a fellow working mother, was repeating the same insensitive and biased words of her privileged white male supervisor that suggested that working was a choice. I thought perhaps that she, as a white woman, got it like that but as for me and my house, our money was *funny* and our change was *strange*. But I assured her that I would do my best to get the work done with the same amount of excellence and integrity I was known for.

I thought we were good—until I received a verbal write-up.

I had never received a write-up in my entire career. My supervisor tried to assure me that the verbal write-up was not the same as an *actual* write-up but rather a way to document her concerns. I wasn't convinced. It was a write-up that was going in my employee record and would have consequences later on. I had been around long enough to see senior Black leaders lose their positions for the same foolishness that their white colleagues got away with. But I am smarter than I look and I cover my ass (CMA) well. The write-up put me in full CMA mode.

If you've ever been in a situation at work where you believed that you needed to cover yourself, you will feel what I am about to say—the shit is exhausting. Hypervigilance and paranoia kick in where suddenly you notice and question everything and anything. Was that comment directed at me? Is there a tone in this email? Who else knows what's going on? Is she actin' funny? You also feel alone and isolated. I started questioning who actually had my back. People who were normally friendly seemed distant. Or maybe it was me? It was hard to know for certain, but what I did know was that I didn't feel safe anymore.

I don't want to assume that you've ever had to cover your ass at work, but if you did, I want you to reflect on how that experience affected you personally and professionally. What impact did the experience have on your mental and physical health? What impact did that experience have on your work performance? And what helped you to navigate through that experience (or helps you if you are going through this now)?

The time for my annual performance review rolled around. Now, for me, performance reviews were generally positive non-events. The ratings often aligned with my own self-evaluation of my performance, and when my ratings increased yearly, so did my salary. This year my review would take place over the phone with my direct supervisor and another supervisor, whose team I worked with but whom I did not report to directly. A copy of the review was emailed twenty minutes before we were scheduled to meet, which was hardly enough time for me to review closely, but plenty of time to see that my overall score had dropped significantly. In one year, my rating decreased from 4.8 out of 5 to a 3.4 out of 5. I was no longer exceeding their expectations. Apparently, I was barely meeting them. Needless to say, the call didn't go well.

I was not in the mood for small talk or pleasantries. I needed answers. I questioned how it was possible that my performance rating could decrease by a whole level, and challenged the accuracy of their rating. I expressed what I believed were more accurate ratings and where there was mutual agreement, I said so. I let them know I was upset because the review wasn't fair, and expected them to do something about it. The other supervisor, someone whom I'd worked with for several years in Memphis and had a great deal of respect for, commandeered the conversation. "Tammy, the bottom line is that you may not agree with what we came up with, but we think your review is fair. I know you're an *overachiever* but a three is actually good."

I was hot! First, there was nothing they could say that justified the low performance scores because to me they reflected minor adjustments to a new location, new teams, and new schedules. The quality of my work had not changed. Second, I felt disrespected. Have you ever been bottom-lined in a disagreement? When somebody tells you, "The bottom line is…" they are basically trying to shut you up and shut you down. That's a no for me. And it was definitely a no for me coming from two white female supervisors trying to convince me that I wasn't the rock star that I knew I was. More than anything it was the statement "you're an overachiever" that really had me in my feelings. In essence, that statement and the low rating symbolized that I was doing too much and needed to be put in my place.

Reflect on a time where you received a similar message (implicitly or explicitly) at work. How was the message that you were doing too much *because you were a Black woman* communicated? Was it a look? A comment? A reaction? How did that messaging make you feel?

A fight for your dignity and worth does not and should not make you an ingrate.

The days following the meeting were a whirlwind because I was in that weird space between needing to fight for my name and reputation and needing to keep my job, wanting to advocate for myself but not wanting to appear ungrateful. I hate that space. A fight for your dignity and worth does not and should not make you an ingrate. But when you're viewed through the prism of Mammy, you're expected to be nappy, happy, and damn sure not snappy. I decided that fighting for my name and reputation was a worthy fight that I was willing to lose.

I responded by challenging the legitimacy of the performance review. I had been a C student before. I wasn't tripping on score alone. I knew I was being treated unfairly. In my written response, I argued that it was the supervisors' obligation to support my performance by identifying not only challenges but also their plans to help me overcome those challenges. I concluded that in the absence of evidence to support the performance review and absence of evidence that they provided support, I believed that I was being discriminated against as a Black woman. I was drawing a line in the sand, and there was no crossing back over to the other side. But it was my truth, and at worst, it would set me free.

I didn't know how to navigate my professional relationship with or my feelings about these two women. I felt betrayed and hurt. I broke bread with these women. One of them attended both my baby and wedding showers as well as my wedding. I was struggling with how to play on a team with teammates that I no longer trusted. I knew how to be cordial and professional, but the way my personality is set up, I can't hide what I feel, and if I ain't feeling you, you will know it. I wasn't feeling them. I also knew HR was going to be involved because of the discrimination complaint in my written response. In effect, that meant that I could not go to HR with my concerns because they were there to protect the company, not me. And then there was the all-too-important matter of what all of this could mean for my family.

Financially, we were struggling. Our incomes decreased significantly with the move, and with the addition of $1,000 monthly in childcare expenses, we were barely making it. And although I did not know exactly what was going to happen at work, I knew eventually I would have to leave. It was hard to imagine any circumstance where it would be business as usual. I was convinced they would fire me or I would resign. And even though my husband was supportive, I felt guilty that I would be to blame for my family's financial disruption.

Then there was the nagging thought that I could be wrong about the whole thing. Maybe their assessment of my performance was valid, and I was just overreacting? But I knew I wasn't. And the word "overachiever" was my clue. In the days following the review, I did some research, which yielded that the word "overachiever" was a stereotype of high-achieving Black women. Further, according to Title VII of the Civil Rights Act of 1964, if my performance review was in fact based on negative stereotypes of Black women, then their actions were unjustified and unlawful.[1]

GOING TO BATTLE

On August 5, 2012, I marched myself down to the local Equal Employment Opportunity Commission (EEOC) office to file a charge of discrimination. The intake person explained to me that although they received hundreds of complaints a month, few of those complaints led to the EEOC filing charges of discrimination because in most cases people failed to prove that discrimination actually occurred. I understood that because I know that for Black folks sometimes all we have is that feeling—it's the feeling you get when you know you're being treated differently because you're Black. You can't always prove it, but you *know*. I assured her that I not only knew, but I could also prove it.

I told her that I was written up for behaviors that other white employees engaged in and when I challenged the write-up with my supervisors, they retaliated by giving me a low performance review. I shared that a white female colleague with my same title told me that she received approval from the state director of our office to work from home several days a week because she didn't have someone to walk her dog during the day or enough gas money to come to work. I explained that the fact that I was written up for working from home with a doctor's order to keep my sick child home, yet my white female colleague had approval to work from home because she didn't have money for gas or dog-walking services, was clearly an example of racial discrimination.

I also shared that the write-up and review highlighted concerns with failure to meet my quarterly training obligations due to frequent schedule conflicts. However, I shared with the intake worker that I had copies of emails between me, my co-trainer, who was a white female, and my two supervisors that proved that it was in fact my co-trainer who had the schedule conflicts, not me. I reiterated my belief to the intake worker that when I expressed to my supervisor that I felt targeted because I was a Black woman, I was subsequently given a low performance review in retaliation for my earlier claims.

After a series of questions, the intake person expressed that she believed that I had established reasonable evidence for my claims but that I would need to speak to a supervisor who would make the final determination of a charge of discrimination. The next thing I heard was the sound of loud footsteps heading toward the direction where I was waiting. Something about the pace and sound of the footsteps suggested that the person meant business—and that I was the person whose business they were coming to handle. For some reason, a scene from *The Color Purple* came to mind—when Sofia blazed through the field to confront Celie about telling Harpo to beat her.

A Black woman appeared in the doorway. The woman introduced herself as the supervisor, and I was immediately put off by her disposition and tone. She seemed irritated, but of course I had no way of knowing whether it was about me or something or someone else. However, I read mood and 'tude for a living, so I could tell that something was up. Keeping on script, she advised me that claims of discrimination did not always lead to charges because they were hard to prove, blah, blah, blah. I let her know that the intake counselor had thoroughly explained that to me and that I was clear about what to expect.

Then the interrogation started. How did I know that one action was the result of another? How could I be sure that my interpretation of the events was accurate? Again, I understood the rationale for this. Alleging that a business violated your civil rights is alleging a federal crime. The EEOC needs tangible proof that your rights have been violated. But what "Sofia" didn't know was that this high achiever had done her homework. I read the laws, cross-referenced them with my experience, and had proof that what happened to me was nothing short of plain old discrimination. By the time I was finished arguing my case, Sofia gave the approval to file a charge of racial discrimination against my employer and advised me that the employer would receive notification of the charges within ten business days.

Those next ten days were emotional. On the one hand, I was afraid. I am conflict avoidant, and fighting is not something I like to do. But I was fighting for my reputation and my rights. On the other hand, I also felt guilt about fighting with a company that had invested so much in me. Was I being ungrateful? Was I making this out to be more than it was? Then there was the hypervigilance. I didn't know when HR would receive the charge and how or if I would be notified, which also made me paranoid. Again, I struggled to know what my interactions should look like with these two women and, more importantly, wondered how would things change.

I agreed to have the EEOC facilitate an in-person mediation with my supervisor in Charlotte to express my concerns and determine an appropriate course of action. The meeting would also be an opportunity to look my supervisor in the eyes and let her know how she failed me as a supervisor and the impact of her actions. I was ready! What I was not ready for was the toll that this experience had on my body. Between proving my case and protecting my name, I failed to recognize the signals my body was sending—that mentally and physically, I was not okay. The trauma of discrimination was taking a toll. Reliving the events. Maintaining hypervigilance. The avoidance. The emotional and physical changes—the signs were all there.

At work, I was anxious every time I had to meet with my supervisor. I couldn't focus, and my heart would beat so loud I was sure she could hear it through the phone. My supervisor seemed to be doing her best to be diplomatic, but it just became too hard to go through the motions with an EEOC complaint against her. I didn't trust her, and she didn't trust me.

Outside of the weekly phone meetings with her and the other supervisor, whom I was now meeting with separately at my request, my contact with them was minimal. With my office door closed, I could cry if I needed to or simply be left alone. Some days that worked. Other days, being in the office was emotionally unbearable.

The mental strain was more evident outside of work. I struggled at school, because unlike work, I couldn't hide behind a phone. And while my professors were somewhat understanding, their motto was "You're a doc student," which basically meant I was expected to get the work done regardless of what was happening in my personal life. My attempts to hold it together didn't always work. One day, I had an unprovoked emotional breakdown during a class lecture. Mentally, it was clear that I was not okay.

As things amped up with the EEOC charge, so did my drinking. My favorite drinking spot was a deli where I could grab a bottle of wine and a sandwich, and hear an occasional DJ set while working on my dissertation. Over time one bottle became two bottles, and "working" at the deli became me commiserating on the phone with my mother about the latest work drama.

One night I was at the spot doing my usual thing when a Black woman sitting at an adjacent table struck up a conversation. I had already been there for a few hours and had polished off at least one or maybe two bottles of wine. We talked—and drank—for several hours that night. At some point, I remember ending the conversation and going to my truck.

The next thing I remember is waking up in the driver's seat to a frantic phone call from my mother. "Tammy?!"

"Yes?"

"Girl, where you at? Juan and I have been calling you for hours. Why didn't you pick up the phone?"

"Ma, I must have fallen asleep. I'm in my car in front of the spot. What time is it?"

"It's four o'clock in the morning. I thought you were dead, girl. Call your husband!"

I did not want to call my husband. Not because I didn't want him to know I was okay, but because I didn't want him to know that I had fallen asleep drunk at the wheel. But I made the call and eventually made my way home. I apologized and assured him that that would not happen again. But I was so disappointed and ashamed that I felt I needed another drink to numb the shame.

As my mental health declined, so did my physical health. My hair, eyebrows, and lashes started falling out. I gained about twelve pounds within two to three months, which I am sure was not helped by regularly drinking one to two bottles of wine and vodka. Then there was insomnia. Racing thoughts about the day's events or the persistent feeling that I was doing something wrong kept me up for hours. Between dealing with work and anticipating the EEOC meeting, I grew sicker by the day.

One of the things I've learned from working with Black female clients dealing with workplace stress is that our bodies are often communicating to us that there is something wrong, but either we don't notice the signs or we ignore them. Think about your own experiences of work-related stress. What have you noticed about your body's response to stressful work situations? Where does that stress show up in your body? And more importantly, what do you do about it? These questions are critical reflection points because your body keeps the score. When you fail to listen to and respond to the body's signals of stress such as sleep disruption, headaches, anxiety, and so on, you lose.

At the EEOC mediation, I met with my supervisor, the company attorney, and the chief human resources officer to discuss my concerns and determine the best course of action. I came ready for war but open to peace. I was unwavering in my belief that what happened was unjustified and unlawful, and I had proof. After it became painfully clear that they could neither disprove nor dismiss my claims, the ball was in my court. The EEOC mediator explained what my options were, and it was mutually agreed that I could continue in my position provided I would have a different supervisor—the same white man who made the comment that my supervisor repeated to me about choosing to be a working mother.

One night shortly after the meeting, I was tossing and turning in bed, thoughts racing about the outcome of the mediation. On the surface, things were resolved. I would continue in my position but have a different supervisor, and perhaps things could be okay. However, the reality was that there was no way I could safely and comfortably work with any of these people again. I felt betrayed. I was unwell. And I was exhausted.

But none of that stopped me from worrying about the financial impact that leaving the job would have on my family. How would my husband feel about me wanting to resign? We'd been married for only a couple of years, and he'd proven to be supportive and dependable. But this felt different. Could he hold it down? Would he hold it down? I didn't know. Something in me broke. I jumped out of bed and ran into the living room of our apartment, balled myself up into a fetal position on the sofa, and SOBBED. The betrayal, the fight, the aftermath, the uncertainty... I felt broken.

At some point, my husband got up to adjust the thermostat and heard me crying, so he came into the living room.

"What's wrong?"

"I can't do this."

"Do what?"

Collapsing in his arms I said, "Continue to work there, Juan! I can't do it! It's too much but I keep worrying about how we're going to—"

"Look, if this place has got you like this, then I need you to resign tomorrow!"

"Are you sure? How are we gonna make it?"

"We will figure it out."

Channeling Big Freedia here: *You already know* what I did! I went to work the next day and emailed my two-week notice to my new supervisor. At our final meeting, I thanked him for the opportunity and expressed that regardless of how things were ending, I was proud of my work and had no regrets. I was leaving on my own terms with my dignity, identity, and integrity intact. Game over.

I'd won that fight. But I'd also lost. I'd lost the naivete of believing that my education and position would earn me respect and inoculate me from institutional racism. In the end, being *smart, kind, and important* did not protect me at all. They were the very things that made me a threat.

Unfortunately, my story isn't unique. In the next chapter, we'll explore how experiences like mine continue to happen to Black women at work. My experience is part of a collective experience, in which negative stereotypes restrict the panoramic view of our humanity as complex, dynamic, intersectional, and multidimensional. At the end of the day, stereotypes not only limit us professionally but also hurt us personally.

If you don't take anything else away from this book, I need you to get this: No job is worth sacrificing your humanity, happiness, and health. You are replaceable at work. You are not replaceable at home. Ain't no sense in killing yourself for a position and a few possessions. At work, you've got to know your worth, show your worth, and bring your worth.

Chapter 3

CHANGING THE GAME: WELLNESS AS THE NEW PLAYBOOK FOR THE WORKPLACE

The Black woman's relationship with work is and always has been complicated. As we've explored in previous chapters, my own complicated path began with the messages I received from my grandmother's and mother's work experiences and continued with my own rewarding, and at times painful, experiences. Through my attempt to understand and heal, I got curious about the experiences of other Black women at work. In effect, my "me-search" became my research. But, as I researched the literature on stereotypes and Black women at work, I could not help but notice that the experiences of people like my mother and grandmother were absent; the voices of those women at the bottom of the workplace hierarchy are often shut out, silenced, or ignored in research.

The Black woman's relationship with work is and always has been complicated.

I decided to use my research to amplify the voices and experiences of women like my mother and grandmother to broaden our understanding of our work experiences as Black women.

Specifically, my doctoral research examined the lived experiences of working-class Black women with race and gender stereotypes at work to understand (a) what kind of race and gender stereotypes working-class Black women experience, (b) how experiences of race and gender stereotypes affect them, and (c) how they cope. I'll dig into my study throughout this chapter, to better illustrate key findings, as well as in subsequent chapters to provide you with practical and proven strategies for putting your wellness first. But first things first—how did we get here?

THE ORIGINS OF THE GAME

Black women's work during slavery as field slaves and domestic workers, in addition to negative depictions of them in contemporary media, has led to negative race and gender stereotypes that continue to affect our experiences at work.[1] Sexual and labor exploitation of enslaved Black women and girls created unique work roles based on the intersection of race and gender. As Black women and girls were racial and gender minorities, the conditions of field and domestic work were predicated on Black women's social location as slaves, Black, and female. Further, the conditions in which enslaved Black women were sold, worked, and punished placed Black womanhood in stark contrast to established social conventions of proper and respectable womanhood most notably expressed in white women's concealment of sexuality. However, for Black enslaved women, scant clothing, forced nudity during auctions, public whippings, and rape did not afford them such privacy and protection.

The contrast of Black womanhood and white womanhood and the need to justify increasing numbers of light-complexioned slave children created a need for white slaveholders to shift the gaze and the blame onto Black women. Race and gender stereotypes such as Jezebel and Mammy emerged to justify exploitation of Black women in their work roles as field slaves and domestic workers, respectively. Although you may have devoted some study to this, continuing to learn about the relationship between slavery and race and gender stereotypes can help illuminate the continued effects of slavery on our current work realities and ultimately our well-being.

While a number of stereotypes of Black women exist, some are key to understanding the discussion of our work experiences. Historically, Jezebel, the stereotype of Black women as lascivious and hyper-reproductive, emerged as a way to justify the rape and exploitation of Black women and girls.[2] Today, the effect of the Jezebel stereotype continues to create perceptions that sexualize our experiences at work. One participant in my study, a fifty-two-year-old Black woman who worked in an administrative position, shared:

> A lot of what I experienced was assumptions that there had to be some type of sexual nature to my relationship with my immediate manager for me to be in the position that I was in…there's a lot going way back to the slave days and having lighter skin….[You] were in the house with the master and what was your purpose other than, you know chores?…It was sexual in nature.[3]

This captures what happens when employers discount Black women's accomplishments and when our successes are attributed to sex and not skills. When perceptions rooted in stereotypes are not challenged, they not only prevent us from receiving the appropriate recognition and opportunities we deserve but also can negatively affect our self-identity, self-confidence, self-worth, and ultimately our self-care.

Another of the more pervasive and deleterious stereotypes of Black women is Mammy. Mammy stereotypes Black women as maternal, asexual, loyal, uneducated, dark-skinned, and obese.[4] This stereotype was commonly associated with Black domestic workers to justify slavery and race relationships. As representations of enslaved persons, images of Mammy as loyal and obedient defied beliefs about slaves as aggressive and uncivilized. As the ideal woman, Mammy was the surrogate mistress and mother who could magically nurture and care for white families better than her own.

When perceptions rooted in stereotypes are not challenged, they prevent us from receiving the appropriate recognition and opportunities we deserve.

The challenge of Mammy (and all stereotypes) then and now is that Black women's humanity and contributions at work are disregarded and disrespected. When projected, the Mammy stereotype often leads employers (especially white employers) to expect us to do more at work with less—and be happy about it. As Mammy, we are expected to be the workplace mama who is there to care for everyone and everything and keep it all together.

What makes this stereotype one of the most dangerous to Black women is that, when internalized, Mammy leads us also to believe that we *should* be everything to everyone. Have you found yourself saying yes when you really needed to say no? Do you consistently put others' needs before yours? Do you feel guilty for putting your needs first? Are you the go-to for people you can't go to? If you answered yes to any of these questions, you best believe that you've internalized Mammy. At work and in life, ideals of Mammy lead to expectations that we are selfless, strong, silent, enduring superwomen who *should* be content with and capable of handling whatever comes our way because of some sort of supernatural strength that no other group of people on the planet have. But as you will see, there is a price to pay when we are complicit in our own dehumanization.

My research found that cheap and disposable labor is another type of stereotype, a finding supported by 2020 national data that show on average Black women earn $0.64 compared to $0.79 for white women for every $1.00 that a white man earns.[5] Cheap and disposable labor, the experience of working in lower-status positions with added job responsibilities without proper compensation, limited promotion opportunities, and feeling disposable, was an issue expressed by seven of the twelve participants in my study. A thirty-one-year-old Black woman shared:

> They had me working like I was a coach supervisor and had me training but they didn't want to give me the pay...you're not promoting me but you're still using me and want to pay me chump change...but the people you're promoting don't even know the job. They just walking around and don't care.[6]

A twenty-five-year-old Black woman who worked as a school bus driver said:

> They hired this girl...I was training her on my floor... probably about a month and a half...I didn't suspect that I was really training her because they knew they were [about to] fire me...I was training her on the floor with me teaching her everything...she was going to be my replacement...when they fired me, she took over

the floor...I mean I trained a couple of people before. I [was thinking] they put the [trainees] with the best people who can train so...I didn't think she was really there to replace me.[7]

These quotes illustrate an experience that many know well—in which one of your duties was "to be determined" and it was determined that you would have the duties of ten people and not be paid for them. Further, that being overworked and underpaid was something you should be happy about. And if you are being honest, at times you believed them. But when you are cheap and disposable labor at work but the Bank of America at home, it is stressful as hell. For many Black women, financial obligations to our children, other people's children, parents, or family members can add mental and physical strain to an already too heavy load. I see this struggle all too often with many of my clients, as they navigate the stress of not being (paid) enough at work and not having enough at home and, worse yet, beat up on themselves for not managing it all. This is the danger of stereotypes: we buy into false narratives of who we should be and then shame and blame ourselves for who we are not (and never should be).

A VERY PRESENT REALITY

Recent gains by Black women in positions where we've previously been excluded might give the illusion that stereotypes are a thing of the past. For the first time in US history, we have a

Black woman vice president. At the time of writing, two Black women are CEOs of Fortune 500 companies: Roz Brewer, CEO of Walgreens Boots Alliance, and Thasunda Brown Duckett, CEO of TIAA. Turn on the news and it seems like every day there is a new report of a first-time Black woman in a top leadership position. Au contraire, ma chérie!

Race and gender stereotypes continue to create unique professional barriers for Black women. Lean In's 2020 *The State of Black Women in Corporate America* report showed that Black women are underrepresented in leadership positions.[8] Despite the fact that 64 percent of Black women have a desire to lead and influence their company's success, Black women occupy only 1 percent of C-suite and vice president roles. Race and gender were expressed as a barrier to advancement by 49 percent of Black women, a finding that my own research yielded.

For many of us, workplace discrimination is a clear and present reality. The impact of discrimination was evident for all twelve of the participants in my study: Seven participants reported they were terminated, two reported demotions, and three reported unexpected job changes such as transfers or role changes. Further, many of the women reported confusion about the changes because for all they knew, their work mattered at the job. They were the trainers for new staff, the dependable go-tos, the do-gooders—they were, in effect, Mammy.

What complicated these experiences was the fact that participant requests for evidence to justify these job changes were either absent or denied. One participant said:

We didn't know that a full investigation was going on...
they told us at the time that we was fired and that they
was doing an investigation on us—that people wrote
statements on us...you suppose to tell us stuff like
that...you don't supposed to do an investigation without us knowing.[9]

These women concluded what I think most of us would
conclude: If you're viewed as cheap and disposable labor, the status of your job changes unexpectedly, and ain't nobody offering
no justification that makes sense to your head—it's straight-up
discrimination!

On top of everything, Black women have to regularly con-
tend with exclusion. The women in my study saw race and
gender stereotypes as the main reason for exclusion by their
managers and communication networks, especially communication about concerns that would lead to changes in employment.
They also expressed that race and gender differences between
them and their managers, changes in management, and conflict
with managers were all related to being excluded at work.

One participant, speaking on her experience of race and
gender differences between her and her manager, stated, "I don't
think he even wanted me in his inner circle...I see his inner
circle as very small—the same couple of white men." Another
spoke about how new management relationships led her to feel
excluded: "It didn't happen until that white man came in. I think
everything seemed fine until he came...people was complaining

that the white man was firing people for no reason." Further, exclusion from communication about performance concerns or impending work status changes in advance, and denial or refusal to provide evidence led to a sense of institutional secrecy and outsider status and ultimately to suspicions of discrimination. One participant, who had been accused of stealing and was terminated and who was denied access to the video evidence her employer said they had, said:

> Whatever evidence they have, make them show it to you! If they ain't got none, you take their ass to court! Show me what you got on me. Let me see. It's like it's a court of law. You said I did this, let me see the evidence that you have on me doing this. Yeah 'cause if you ain't got none, I'm gon' have to see you in court because it's discrimination.[10]

Race and gender stereotypes create barriers for Black women at work that distort how employers see and treat us. And yet for all of this current discussion about diversity, equity, inclusion, and accessibility (DEIA), the needle has not moved much in terms of Black women reaching a critical mass in top leadership positions and being well when we get there. It's time that businesses stop performing DEIA and actually do the work of becoming anti-racist organizations that see and support the inherent worth and dignity of all employees, but specifically Black women. We have more work to do. It's not enough to celebrate all the glass on the floor with a few wins. We want the glass—or, in the case of Black women, the concrete—ceiling removed completely.

OUR BODIES AT RISK

The fact that these stereotypes create professional barriers for Black women is not new news. As we all know, there is much public and private discourse about the impact of stereotypes that limit hiring, retention, and promotion for Black women. In your own personal life, I am sure you can think of at least one example where you believed that being Black and female was the *real* reason for why you needed to have *the meeting* or didn't get the promotion or opportunity. Yet what is talked about less is what happens to our bodies when we have to constantly navigate experiences of race and gender stereotypes at work.

Playing the game is not only weighty but also costly.[11] When Black women internalize stereotypes, we work harder. The additional labor of asserting our worth and humanity taxes our minds, bodies, and souls. What's worse is when we unconsciously play into new stereotypes to resist the old ones. Belief in notions of the strong Black woman or asserting #BlackGirlMagic is nothing more than white stereotypes in blackface. Because of these, Black women are silently suffering because, although we are allegedly imbued with extraordinary strength, the data indicate otherwise. When Black women play the game, black *does* crack, mentally and physically.

Research shows that experiences of discrimination at work have profound negative consequences on our mental wellness.[12] Specifically, experiences of race and gender stereotypes have been associated with eating disorders, depression, addiction, anxiety, and nervous breakdowns.[13] My own research found emotional and cognitive effects resulting from these experiences at work. Participants reported feeling confused when disciplinary actions were taken because they believed that they were doing their job and doing it well. Thus, when job changes occurred without justifiable reasons for the changes, many of the participants attributed the changes initially to personal shortcomings.

When Black women play the game, black does crack, mentally and physically.

Stereotypes at work don't affect just how we feel but also how we think about ourselves. Half the participants in my study expressed thoughts of self-doubt when unexpected and unjustified changes happened at work. One participant shared, "I [was] beating up on myself like what could I have done better? What could I have done differently?" Another participant said, "You feel bad about that as a person when you're giving everything that you can give into this to make yourself work...you fall back a little 'cause you feel like am I worth it? Can I do it?" Similarly, one participant shared, "I allowed that [experience] to seep into my psyche and I started doubting myself." Thus, as these quotes illustrate, we cannot afford to be ill-equipped with antiquated messaging that is both a by-product and producer of the very stereotypes that are making us mentally unwell. It is necessary for us to be armored with tools that help us prioritize our minds *and* our money.

If the data on the mental health effects of these workplace experiences are concerning, then the data on the physical effects are even more alarming—and get ready, because this is a lot. Experiences of race and gender stereotypes at work have been identified as a chronic source of stress for us. Heart disease and cancer are the number one and number two leading causes of death of Black women in the US, respectively.[14] While biological determinants partly explain rates of disease in Black women, social determinants such as experiences of stereotypes and workplace discrimination also contribute significantly to negative physical health outcomes.

In 2012, researchers J. Camille Hall, Joyce Everett, and Johnnie Hamilton-Mason conducted a study investigating Black women's workplace stress and coping and found that experiences of race and gender stereotypes in the workplace were associated with stress, sleep deprivation, hair loss, hypertension, diabetes, and weight gain.[15] Others have also found neurological disorders such as migraine headaches to be associated with experiences of stereotypes at work. We also see a relationship between workplace stress and adverse reproductive health outcomes in Black women. Yet again, because of ideas that posit Black women as strong and impervious to harm, some of us suffer in silence when it comes to our reproductive health. In 2018, Womens HealthMag.com and OprahMag.com surveyed one thousand women regarding infertility issues and found that Black women are almost twice as likely to experience infertility compared to white women but because of stigma and bias are less likely to discuss issues with infertility.[16] However, the public discourse on this issue is growing thanks to folks like Michelle Obama, Serena Williams, and Meghan Markle talking openly about their fertility issues. Thus, because this issue disproportionately affects Black women, it is critical that we shine a light on factors such as workplace stress that contribute to this health crisis.

WHAT'S TO COME

As a wellness issue, our experiences of race and gender stereotypes at work highlight the need for a new career playbook, one that offers practical strategies to help us prioritize self-care and self-empowerment as necessary rules of the game—the new game—where the main objective is being well while we excel. The remaining chapters are designed to help you do just that. In chapters 4–7 you will learn self-care strategies that help you manage your stress and maintain your sanity. In chapters 8–10, you will learn self-empowerment strategies to help you be aware of, affirm, and advocate for your worth at work. Each chapter will provide practical steps to achieve each skill as well as helpful tips that provide additional considerations. Before you proceed, please note that the strategies in this book neither constitute nor substitute for a professional counseling relationship. But, if you need tips on how to find help, I got you covered. Chapter 5 will include tips for how to find a mental health professional.

Beginning with chapter 4, you will also learn key strategies to help you take care of the one car you will ever have to navigate this life—your body. In chapter 5, you will learn strategies that promote mental clarity and emotional stability to help you get—and keep—your mind right. Chapter 6 will teach you strategies to help you know your worth and stand in your truth. Chapter 7 provides strategies to set professional boundaries that help you know your lane and stay in it. In chapter 8, you'll learn how to identify whether the people in your circle are in your corner and how to find and ask for help when you need it. Chapter 9 will provide you strategies for getting somebody together—without snatching them up. Finally, chapter 10 will offer decision-making strategies to know when it's time to stand your ground and when it's time to throw 'em the deuces.

We're changing the game and the narrative with this one, y'all! Leggo!

Chapter 4

TAKE CARE OF THE BASICS

Currently, self-care is trendy. Everybody, from entertainers and athletes to influencers and regular everyday folks, is talking about self-care. While opinions vary on what self-care is, what it has become synonymous with are luxuriating facials, manis and pedis, and long bubble baths. Effectively, self-care is seen as self-indulgent. But for some Black women, self-care is an act of resistance; the thinking is that when a Black woman prioritizes self-care, it means she's sticking it to the man. If you happen to fall in this group, I hate to burst your bubble—self-care is not revolutionary. It is essential. It is basic. It is the daily activity of caring for your mind-body-spirit so that you can survive and thrive. As such, self-care is the very thing that you need to breathe and be.

At its basic level, self-care means taking care of your mental and physical health. Repeat after me: "Mental health *is* physical health and physical health *is* mental health." If you get only one message from this chapter, I need to you to understand that you cannot be mentally well if you are physically unwell. They go together like red beans and rice.

Mental health *is* physical health and physical health *is* mental health.

However, when you are dealing with situations at work in which perceptions and treatment of you are rooted in race and gender stereotypes, your self-care is usually the first thing to go. You're not sleeping as much. You might be eating too much and too much of the wrong things. You might be drinking too much—alcohol, that is. You're not working out or getting physical activity as much. Spiritually, you may be disconnected or discouraged. So let this rest in your spirit: Taking care of yourself is nonnegotiable!

Regardless of what is going on at work, there are basic things your body needs: sleep, food, water, and movement. At best, neglecting those needs leaves you underprepared to effectively navigate work and, at worst, puts your health and life at risk. No job is worth you being sick or dying. Not one![1] Thus, self-care is a necessary component for navigating work.

In this chapter, our goal is to help you take better care of you by addressing some of the wellness issues most affected by our experiences of race and gender stereotypes at work. These areas and the tools within may seem basic, but they are the cornerstones of wellness and where we must begin before moving on to the deeper work.

PRIORITIZE SLEEP

According to the National Sleep Foundation, adults ages eighteen to sixty-four and those sixty-five and older need an average of seven to nine hours of sleep and seven to eight hours of sleep, respectively.[2] However, 33 percent of the adult population is sleep deprived. So, "turn down for what?" you ask Lil Jon. Like my husband and I tell our ten-year-old, "Because you need to go your butt to bed!" If your computer has a sleep mode that helps to preserve its power and resume normal operations when the sleep function is disabled, then surely sleep helps you in the same way.

There are several factors that may explain why we are not sleeping. Sometimes sleep deprivation is a symptom of mental health conditions (e.g., depression and anxiety), physical health conditions (e.g., stress, sleep apnea), or environmental conditions (e.g., a bright room, noise). For Black women, our struggles in the workplace are unique stressors that make us more susceptible to sleep deprivation. Yet sleep deprivation leads to a number of mental health issues; for example, sleep deprivation is associated with stress, anxiety, irritability, and fatigue. It also impairs your ability to regulate your mood and emotions and make sound decisions. In essence, when you don't get enough sleep, your body is in threat mode, not thrive mode. And we want you to thrive, so having tools to help you sleep more is critical. The steps below are intended to promote sleep hygiene that can lead to increased healthy sleep.

Limit Sleep Disrupters

Noise, lights from electronics, alcohol, and caffeine can disrupt your ability to go to sleep and stay asleep. For many of us, sleep disrupters are intended to be sleep inducers. I've worked with clients who for various reasons were afraid to sleep in complete darkness, so they kept their televisions on to avoid it. I must admit I was one of those people. It took years of therapy to work through trauma to be able to sleep in the dark and not be afraid. Yet lights emitted from television and electronics disrupt our body's sleep cycle, so avoid that by turning off the TV, shutting down your electronic devices, and shutting down social media at least one hour before bedtime. However, if you do need some light in your room, night-lights are an effective alternative to the television.

Also, avoid the use of alcohol and caffeine prior to bedtime. Many of my clients have reported alcohol use as a form of self-medication for insomnia, anxiety, or other mental and physical health conditions. That glass of wine before bed sounds nice and may even help you go to sleep, but too many glasses of wine (i.e., four glasses for women) will disrupt your ability to get REM sleep, which is the level of sleep you need to wake up and feel rested. One healthy alternative to alcohol is the use of aromatherapy. Lavender oil use at nighttime has been shown to promote sleep and calm. Diffusing lavender oil, spraying lavender on your linens, or applying lavender oil to your wrists and temples can not only help you go to sleep but also improve the quality of your sleep. Other healthy alternatives include reading or listening to books, meditation, and mindfulness practices.

Stick to a Consistent Sleep Routine and Schedule

Establishing a consistent sleep routine and schedule helps you wind down and signals to your body that it is bedtime. First, identify at least one or two relaxing sleep routines (e.g., taking a warm bath, reading, listening to relaxing music or sounds, or prayer and meditation). I recommend you start your sleep routine at least one hour before bedtime to prepare your mind and body for sleep. Second, identify a time each night that allows you to get the recommended minimum of seven hours of sleep. Adjust if you need more than the recommended seven hours, but try to get at least seven hours. You'll know you've had enough sleep if you can wake up without the use of an alarm and feel rested.

Limit the Use of Your Bed for Activities Other Than Sleep

Getting into bed at bedtime helps your body to relax and prepare for sleep. Using your bed as a work or study space makes it difficult for your brain to associate your bed with sleep time. Therefore, try to limit bed use to those times when you are going to sleep (and sex, of course—can't forget sex!).

STRESS LESS

Have you ever heard the saying "Whatever doesn't kill you makes you stronger"? Maybe you've even said it. But let me be clear about what does kill you: stress! I'ma say it again—stress kills. And if it doesn't kill you, it definitely makes you sick. The research is replete with links between stress and adverse health outcomes.[3] Stress is associated with cancer, hypertension, heart disease, diabetes, depression, addiction, anxiety, hair loss, and migraines, among other conditions. Not surprisingly, these are also health issues that Black women experience as they navigate instances of race and gender stereotypes at work. Black women are sick and dying, figuratively and literally, simply because of our race and gender. Our very existence is stressful.

Damn.

But I want you to know that regardless of the stress and chaos around you, you have the ability to let stress not get the best of you. The techniques offered below are intended to promote inner calm and relaxation—whenever and wherever you need them.

TECHNIQUES FOR DEVELOPING INNER CALM

Ujjayi Breathing

- Get in your power position: Sit with your back straight, feet firmly beneath you, and place your hands, palms up, on your lap.
- Close your eyes and inhale slowly through your nose for a four-count (i.e., counting 1-2-3-4 silently in your head).
- Hold your breath for a three-count (counting 1-2-3 silently in your head).
- Exhale through your mouth for a five-count (counting 1-2-3-4-5, allowing the sound of your breath to come out).
- Repeat these steps three times or until you feel calm and relaxed. Repeat as often as you need to throughout the day.

Mindfulness Meditation

- Get in your power position: Sit with your back straight, feet firmly beneath you, and place your hands, palms up, on your lap.

- Close your eyes and inhale slowly through your nose and exhale through your mouth.
- After three full breaths (inhaling and exhaling fully three times), direct your attention to your breath by noticing how it is moving in and out of your body.
- If thoughts or noise distractions occur, do not judge or focus on them but bring your focus back to your breathing. Continue to notice how your breath is moving through your body.
- Repeat these steps as often as you need to throughout the day.

Grounding: 5-4-3-2-1 Technique

- Get in your power position: Sit with your back straight, feet firmly beneath you, and place your hands, palms up, on your lap.
- Working backward from five, name:
  - Five things you see (e.g., I see my plant, I see my clock, I see my computer, I see my lamp, I see the door). It's okay to notice the small things. The point is not *what* you notice but rather *that* you notice.
  - Four things you hear (e.g., I hear the radio, I hear the hum of my fan, I hear yard work, I hear my sound machine).
  - Three things you feel (e.g., I feel my bottom on the seat, I feel my feet on the floor, I feel my clothes against my skin).

- Two things you smell (e.g., I smell my candle burning, I smell my perfume).
- One thing you taste (e.g., I taste coffee).

HELPFUL TIPS

- Don't stress over doing techniques designed to help you de-stress. Proficiency requires practice, patience, self-compassion, and nonjudgment.
- Use these techniques whenever and wherever to decrease stress and promote relaxation.
- If self-practice is challenging, there are a number of no-cost and paid apps that provide guided practice, such as Calm, Insight Timer, and Headspace.

STAY HEALTHY

You have the power to make choices that lead to a healthy life. Remember that, because the things that you experience as a Black woman can make you feel helpless to exercise choice. Systemic barriers such as medical discrimination and lack of access to high-quality, affordable health care have real implications for our well-being. Navigating these barriers can be overwhelming and disempowering and can limit our agency to make choices that promote our wellness. But navigating these systemic barriers alone is not the reason we are leading in mortality rates due to heart disease and cancer.

Some of those outcomes are because of our lifestyle choices—or the lack thereof. When we choose to put everybody before our own body, our health suffers. When we choose to eat foods that are high in sugar, salt, fat, and chemicals, our health suffers. When we don't engage in physical activity or exercise, our health suffers. When we don't have routine exams, our health suffers. I want you to feel empowered by the fact that you still have choice in the midst of constraints. Yes, those constraints might require you to do a bit more to ensure that your oxygen mask is on, but you are worth the extra effort. When it comes to being there for others, we make a way out of no way. I know you do. I've been there myself. I have bent myself into knots being the go-to for others only to find out that those same people were not go-tos for me.

When we choose to put everybody before our own body, our health suffers.

You know where else we do a lot of back bending? You guessed it—at work! Working twice as hard. Breaking your back to make somebody else's dream happen because you believe that's what you are supposed to do. And then being too exhausted when you come home to work on your own dreams. Time out for that! Your health is your wealth.

I want you to know that you can choose health and take steps that are within your control to be healthy. Remember, you always have a choice. Thus, the steps offered below are intended to help you make choices to get on—and stay on—your path to be the healthiest version of yourself.

Eat Better

Food is mood. Eat food that is good for you and not just good to you. Consuming foods rich in omega-3 fatty acids (like salmon, flax, and chia seeds), whole grains (such as brown rice and quinoa), green veggies (like spinach and broccoli), nuts and seeds (like almonds and peanuts), and vitamin D–rich foods (like milk and cheese—if you're not vegan) are critical for your physical and mental well-being.[4] Eating healthier is a process that takes planning and preparation.

And if you are like me, eating healthier also takes support and accountability. Have you ever had that moment when you saw yourself in a picture and you asked, "Where did all this weight come from?" If this is not your testimony, bless you. Unfortunately, it is my testimony and the testimony of many Black women. The first time I asked myself that question and did something about it was in 2007 when, at thirty-one years old, I weighed the most that I'd ever weighed. And I didn't feel healthy. I was fortunate enough to work for a company that had a workout room with a fitness trainer and Weight Watchers meetings on-site. I committed to getting healthier and within a year lost fifty-three pounds. The second time I asked myself that question was in 2021, after seeing myself in a picture I'd taken after a radio interview I gave for a local talk show. My excitement about taking a picture with one of the hosts, a legendary news anchor and journalist, was overshadowed by the fact that I was bigger than I realized. A doctor's visit following the interview confirmed that somehow, I was the largest I'd been in my adult life. That time led me to work with a certified fitness trainer, whose interview I'd heard on the same talk radio show. In addition to personal training with her three days a week, my fitness plan includes a weekly meal plan with intermittent fasting; after four months, I can happily say that, as of this writing, I have shed forty pounds!

Be honest with yourself. If you need support and accountability for eating healthier, consider working with fitness professionals who provide meal programs, nutritionists, or dietitians who can help you build and maintain healthy eating habits. Of course, working with professionals is an investment—one that you are worth. But start with what you can afford. Many fitness professionals have hourly rates and fitness packages suitable to a range of budgets, so do your research. Also, nutrition and dietetics may be covered benefits under your health insurance, so check your coverage.

If you are a do-it-yourselfer, planning and preparation work best. Make it easy for yourself. Smoothies, meal prep, or meal prep/meal kit services can help to ensure you are consuming the nutrients your body needs to function optimally. Start small. Making just one of your meals healthier makes a big difference. Try alternating a healthy mealtime each week: first week, healthy breakfast; second week, healthy lunch; third week, healthy dinner; and repeat. Once you get in the habit, this will be easier to do. Remember, the cost of not eating healthier is greater.

Stay Hydrated

You don't need Method Man to survive (a nod to my friend in my head, Mary J. Blige), but you definitely need water. There is not an organ, cell, or tissue in your body that does not need water to function properly. Drinking water helps with mood, headaches, weight, and digestion.[5] I recommend keeping a refillable cup that you can fill up throughout the day with water. If you don't enjoy drinking water, okay, I hear you. Try infusing water with slices of fruit (e.g., lemon, oranges, cucumbers) or with mint leaves to enhance the flavor to boost your water intake. The more you drink water, the more your body will start to crave it. Trust me on this.

Stay Active

Regular exercise is proven to have a number of mental and physical health benefits. Just thirty minutes of exercise three times a week can improve mood, decrease anxiety, decrease stress, and increase self-confidence. If it's easier, it's okay to break down the thirty minutes into smaller ten-minute increments each day. There are a range of physical activities you can do, some of which you may already be doing. If so, wonderful—keep it up! If you have not started, consult with your physician and a certified fitness professional on activities that may work for you. But generally, an activity such as brisk walking a few times a week does your body good. Most importantly, find exercise that you enjoy doing—that way, you're more likely to keep it up.

Wherever you are on this aspect, know that your mindset matters. Keep a goal or focus in mind for your physical activity to keep you on track. For example, I am clear that I work out to not lose my mind, not to lose weight. The fact that I am sad and short with people when I don't work out is just the motivation I need to get going when I want to lie in bed a bit longer in the morning. Setting SMART (specific, measurable, achievable, relevant, and time-specific) goals can help you stay focused and moving.

So let's say you decided that you would get active by working out. Using the SMART framework, you might come up with a goal such as "I will walk in the park for thirty minutes, three times a week for the next thirty days."

- Specific: Specific goals are easy to understand. "Working out" is vague. But in the example, walking in the park is the specific activity that will be done.

- Measurable: Measurable goals are numerical and therefore trackable. In the example, it is easy to track a thirty-minute walk, three times a week.

- Achievable: Achievable goals are based on what you can do (and will do). Honesty with yourself is key. In the example, "achievable" is represented by walking in the park for thirty minutes, three times a week. It goes without saying, but I'm saying it: The assumption is that you can walk and your schedule allows for, or rather you make allowances for, a thirty-minute walk, three times a week.

- Relevant: Relevant goals are motivational in nature and based on where you are and what you are trying to accomplish. In our example, walking is a form of working out that, pain or discomfort notwithstanding, many people find enjoyable.

- Time-specific: Time-specific goals have an end point or deadline. In the example, thirty days is the time frame in which the walking will occur.

Stay Current on Annual Exams

Physical health symptoms can sometimes mimic mental health symptoms. For example, fatigue can be a symptom of depression, but it can also be a symptom of vitamin D deficiency or thyroid disease, among other things. Physical health symptoms can also exacerbate mental health symptoms. Therefore, stay current on your annual well-woman and physical exams. It's important to get both—every year. (If you are due for either of your exams right now—stop reading and go schedule them—real talk!)

And while getting annual exams is critical, it is also important to acknowledge the barriers that we often experience in health care. Stereotypes, bias, and medical discrimination create significant challenges to Black women seeking and receiving adequate health care. Many counseling sessions have been spent processing my clients' experiences in which they felt dismissed or ignored during their doctors' visits. That's if they could get through the door and to an actual appointment. Sometimes our session time was spent processing barriers to scheduling or navigating health insurance claims. In either instance, my clinical focus involved not only validating and normalizing their feelings but also coaching them through persistence in finding a culturally responsive health care provider. And advocating for their health needs when they do. Advocating for oneself as a Black woman can be difficult, again, because of internalized race and gender stereotypes that cause us to minimize our own needs and concerns at the expense of our health and happiness.

So, at your annual exams, talk with your physician about anything that you are noticing is not right—a bump, a lump, a pain, a strain—whatever it is, tell 'em. Request lab work during your annual visits to ensure everything internally is functioning optimally. Some of us live with something wrong with us because we are supposed to be strong. Take a licking and keep on ticking, right? Wrong! Failing to prioritize your health is not a measure of strength. It is a badge of dishonor. Your body is your temple. Honor it and take care of it!

HELPFUL TIPS

- Find an accountability partner to help you stay motivated and on track.
- Knowing what to do is half the battle, so seek professional support when necessary.
- Remember that wellness is a journey, not a destination! Have some grace for your pace!

CONNECT TO THE SPIRIT

Spirituality has many definitions but is defined here as *that which gives you meaning and purpose*. Spirituality in its basic form encompasses a set of beliefs and behaviors that guide a sense of meaning and purpose. For Black women, spirituality is also an evidence-based source of self-care, self-empowerment, and coping for dealing with experiences of race and gender stereotypes at work.[6] Research shows that a belief in a higher power or purpose greater than themselves helps Black women to cope effectively with their race-and-gender-stereotype-related work experiences, a finding that other researchers also confirmed.[7]

However, as a clinician, I am also aware that spirituality or, specifically, religion can be a real source of pain, confusion, and trauma for some Black women. Many of my queer clients report being traumatized by messages that they were evil and going to hell because of their affectional status or gender identity. This trauma was compounded when family members and loved ones also believed that same messaging. There is also the painful and confusing schism that occurs when Black women develop a spiritual identity that may be different from the one from their childhood as they examine for themselves what is real and true. Further, when negative experiences happen to us, we may even question our faith in search of understanding and meaning. And yet for some Black women, spirituality is not a salient aspect of their identity at all.

Like most things, spirituality exists on a continuum. If you believe in something greater than yourself that gives you meaning and purpose, I respect that. If you don't believe, I respect that too. However, spirituality is an evidence-based source of self-care, self-empowerment, and coping for Black women dealing with race and gender stereotypes at work. Thus, the following steps are intended to help you create purpose and meaning.

Maintain a Panoramic View of Spirituality

Broaden your understanding of the concept of spirituality. Spirituality is an individual, personal, and sometimes lonely search for *your* truth and ultimately *the* truth. It is okay, then, if your spiritual beliefs and practices break from your childhood or family traditions. It is okay if you subscribe to one spiritual practice, a mix of practices, or none at all. It is okay to research, read, and immerse yourself in different spiritual practices to develop a spiritual identity that is uniquely yours. But keep in mind, some people—*your* people—may not like it. They may not agree with it. It may not make sense to them. That's okay too. But your spiritual beliefs and practices do need to make sense to you—and *work* for you.

Prioritize Your Spiritual Practices Daily

I am going to keep this one really simple. If your spiritual practices work for you, do them and devote more time to them. Consistent spiritual practice yields consistent positive results. My personal and clinical experiences have shown me that consistent use of spiritual practices has positive effects on mood, emotional regulation, and coping. Conversely, consistent spiritual practice that is not working for you yields negative results. If you are engaging in spiritual practices that don't work for you, you should examine why you still do them. Doing something that doesn't work will hurt you in the long run.

If your spiritual practices work, prioritize them in your daily life. Build your practices into your schedule and protect that time. My alarm is set for 6:00 a.m. every day so I can pray and say positive affirmations before everyone else in my household wakes up. For me, it is important to start my day in prayer and communion with God and to get armored up for the workday.

Whatever your thing is—prayer, gratitude, meditation, crystals, talking to the ancestors—do that every day. Your spiritual practices are your protective gear. Stay armored up! Pray, if that's your thing, and get professional counseling to bolster your spirituality.

HELPFUL TIPS

- Spirituality is a deeply personal experience. The key is figuring out what spiritual practices work for *you*.
- Spirituality, like most things, works best when you practice it consistently.
- If you don't know God, try him! If it doesn't work, you can always go back to what you were doing.

Chapter 5

PROTECT YOUR PEACE

Maybe you're wondering why a chapter about mental health is titled "Protect Your Peace." On the surface, I suspect the reasons seem somewhat obvious. I suspect it makes sense that when you are mentally well, you have peace. If you landed here, you would be correct. Yet the act of protecting your peace goes deeper. It is a proclamation that, regardless of what happens at work (and in life), you have a right and a responsibility to prioritize your own peace of mind. Further, protecting your peace is something within your control, and with practice, you can become proficient in it. This is important to understand, especially because the drama and sometimes trauma we experience at work can hinder our sense of agency and ability to take care of ourselves. With the following steps and helpful tips to promote mental clarity and emotional stability, and tips to find a professional counselor if doing it alone is not enough, you will be armored with tools you need to keep your peace.

GAIN MENTAL CLARITY

In my clinical practice, I consistently observe the effect that experiences of race and gender stereotypes at work have on my clients' self-perception and self-worth. The common thread is a tendency for these clients to blame themselves for the ill intentions of their bosses and co-workers, accompanied by a belief that not being good enough was the *real* reason. Over time, negative self-perception and self-worth become an infected wound that festers and affects not only our well-being but also our productivity, relationships, and every aspect of our lives. Viewed from this perspective, the need to protect your peace becomes evident. We can't protect our peace without mental clarity—the ability to view and respond to situations in ways that are healthy and helpful. Mental clarity begins with healthy thoughts. To help my clients, and now you, understand this, I want to introduce you to cognitive behavioral therapy (CBT), a counseling framework that has gained increasing popularity since it was first developed in the 1960s by psychiatrist Aaron T. Beck. This evidenced-based practice has proven to be effective to not only promote mental clarity but also to address a range of mental health conditions associated with experiences of race and gender stereotypes at work, such as anxiety, depression, and trauma. The main tenet of CBT is that change can be arranged when you change how you think. By understanding that your thoughts influence your feelings and ultimately your behaviors, you can gain more control over *stinkin' thinkin'* that hinders your ability to feel in control of your feelings and behaviors.

Avoid the Rabbit Hole—Challenge Negative Thoughts

I teach my clients to think about their thinking, a process called *metacognition*. This is one of the hallmarks of cognitive behavioral counseling frameworks. Most of us are not thinking about our thinking. Further, most of us don't believe we can change or control our thinking. But identifying and challenging negative thoughts is a powerful way to manage your mood and behavior.

With this technique, you'll practice recognizing and replacing untrue, unhealthy, and unhelpful thoughts with thoughts that are true, healthy, and helpful. True thoughts are factual or realistic. Healthy thoughts make you feel good about yourself and the situation and are strength focused. Helpful thoughts help you cope with a situation. Developing this ability can have positive effects on your self-perception, self-worth, and, ultimately, your well-being.

To illustrate, consider April, a client who applied for and was denied a promotion. She thought, "Ah, I didn't deserve the promotion anyway." This statement is patently untrue— she applied for the promotion, which in itself reflects her belief that she deserved one. The thought behind the statement is also unhealthy, because April holding on to the belief that she didn't deserve to be recognized and rewarded for her work certainly does not engender feelings of worth and well-being. This is further unhelpful because it could affect April's future outlook about work. In working to challenge and reframe your negative thoughts, you will avoid slipping down the rabbit hole that leads to negative thinking, feelings, and behaviors because of thoughts that simply are not true, healthy, or helpful.

SELF-REFLECTION EXERCISE

To identify negative thoughts, ask yourself:

- Is this thought true? What evidence do I have that it is true?
- Is this thought healthy? Does the thought make me feel better about myself or the situation?
- Is this thought helpful? Does the thought help me deal with the situation effectively?

To replace negative thoughts, ask yourself:

- What thought could I replace my previous thought with to make it true?
- What is another way I can think about this situation that would make me feel better about myself or the situation?

- What is another way of thinking about this situation that would help me deal more effectively with this situation?

Process:

- Pick a recent or past situation that happened at work and write down the main thought associated with the situation (e.g., "I didn't get the promotion because I didn't deserve it"). Identify what you *thought*, not what you *felt*.
- Now, write down how the thought made you *feel* (e.g., "When I thought I didn't get the promotion because I didn't deserve it, it made me *feel worthless*").
- To identify negative thoughts, reflect on the questions in the first set of self-reflection prompts and write down your answers to each question.
- To replace the negative thoughts, reflect on and write down your answers to the second set of self-reflection prompts.
- After you've answered all the questions in the second set of self-reflection prompts, reflect on and write down your response to the question, "If I had this new thought, how might I feel?" Pay attention to how the new thought would change your feelings about the situation.

- Practice, practice, practice! Practice the steps on work and nonwork experiences to gain proficiency with the skill.

Change Your Perspective

Think of a time when changing your perspective changed how you felt about the situation. Changing your perspective probably made you feel better about the situation even though the situation itself did not change. There's evidence behind that feeling, which makes it a clinically effective tool for promoting mental clarity. Changing your perspective means being clear on your *why* as a tool to navigate experiences related to race and gender stereotypes at work. Your why could be factors that are internal, external, or both. In the study I conducted, every single participant identified that once they were able to change their perspective, they were better able to cope with experiences of race and gender stereotypes at work. One participant said, "I'm a mother. I had no choice. One thing about what I went through—you have to keep your head up." For her, her why was her children. For you, your why might be your faith, your family, your finances, or your future. Your why is *your* truth. And, the truth is, sometimes you have to make work, work. As a therapist, Black woman, and mother—I get that. For some, not working is not an option. Therefore, changing your perspective can give you a sense of control, particularly if there is a tangible or fore-seeable benefit to a changed perspective on work.

I help my clients identify their why by exploring their personal or professional goals (e.g., taking care of family, paying off debt, gaining experience) and steps they could take to achieve their goals. Even if the situation is not the best, I support my clients' autonomy to make choices by creating a safe space for them to explore all of the choices available and to make the choices that work for them. Knowing that you have choices is critical because often we do not believe we have choices, or we are penalized when those choices prioritize us.

When we fail to prioritize our well-being as a *necessary* component of our why, it is ultimately our well-being that takes a back seat.

So, I will tell you like I tell them—whatever your why is, be clear about it. Knowing your why can be your compass to navigate work and your path to wellness. But I also know that we can make our why our crutch. It's easy for Black women to believe that choosing our why over our well-being makes sense because we are expected to be in service to everything and everyone over ourselves. But when we fail to prioritize our well-being as a *necessary* component of our why, it is ultimately our well-being that takes a back seat.

CHANGING YOUR PERSPECTIVE

Let's say you are working in a job that you are unhappy with but are unable to leave. Asking yourself the following questions can help you change your perspective and find peace in the meantime, in-between time.

- What is my *why* in this situation?
  - What personal goals is this job helping me achieve?
    - How long will it take me to achieve my personal goals?
    - What steps do I need to take to achieve my goals?
    - What resources or support will help me achieve my goals?
  - What career goals is this job helping me achieve?
    - How long will it take me to achieve my career goals?
    - What steps do I need to take to achieve my goals?
    - What resources or support will help me achieve my goals?
- What are my options in this situation?
  - Are my options realistic and doable?
  - What steps do I need to make my options possible?
  - What resources or support will I need to make my options possible?
- How will prioritizing my why *help* my well-being?
- How will prioritizing my why *hinder* my well-being?

Process:

- Reflect on and write down your answers to each main self-reflection prompt and its corresponding sub-questions.
- After you've answered all the questions in the self-reflection prompts, reflect on and write down your response to the question, "How can changing my perspective help me navigate future situations at work?"
- Practice, practice, practice! Practice the steps on work and nonwork experiences to gain proficiency with the skill.

MAINTAIN EMOTIONAL STABILITY

Emotional stability, the ability to recognize, respond, and regulate your feelings, is another key aspect of protecting your peace. A note here: I will use "feelings" synonymously with "emotions" throughout the remaining sections. Feelings are our bodies' internal messaging system. Our feelings communicate all sorts of important messages about our needs, wants, physical and psychic threats, and more. Our workplace experiences can pull us through extreme ranges of feeling. It is critical that we listen to what our feelings are telling us about our lives. Unfortunately for many Black women, we not only minimize our feelings, but we also mistrust them. And stereotypes and socialization are partly to blame for this.

I was a crier as a child, and my mama and grammaw fussed over this constantly. I can't remember if I was ever explicitly told that my crying was a sign of weakness, but it was clear that crying was not welcomed. And my mama and grammaw weren't the best models for expressing feelings either. I rarely saw either of them cry unless somebody died. Outside of that, I mostly saw their anger, which they socialized me to believe equaled strength. As the years passed, my crying became more discreet and my anger more pronounced. Apparently, I wasn't the only Black woman who internalized that message.

So often I have to reassure my Black female clients that they don't have to apologize when they cry in their counseling sessions because counseling is meant to be a *safe* container for their tears. One client in particular will repeatedly tell herself, "Don't cry!" in session whenever she starts to (or wants to) cry. I do my absolute best to ensure her and all of my clients that their feelings are safe with me. Yet I am aware that my message is probably the only time or one of a few times that they heard that their tears—their feelings—were safe to express.

Think about the messages you have received about expressing your feelings. What were they and where did they come from? Did you see healthy models in your environment that expressing feelings was acceptable as a Black woman? I suspect you or maybe someone you know didn't always have your feelings acknowledged and affirmed. Further, somewhere along the way you learned that *certain* feelings were okay for you—as a Black woman—to express. And if that is your daily lived experience, then you know how hard it can be to acknowledge and affirm your own feelings.

Given all of this, what do you think happens when you have to show up and deal with an invalidating work environment? I can assure you that what does not happen is that you suddenly become a feelings detective. Our experiences of race and gender stereotypes at work often compound the messages we received outside of work, which together create mental noise that is hard to silence. By not attending to our feelings, we miss critical opportunities to engage in the self-care and self-preservation we need. Listen—you can't tame what you can't name! Thus, developing the skills to recognize and respond to your feelings promotes the emotional stability needed to ensure *healthy* and sustained success at work and beyond.

IDENTIFYING AND RESPONDING TO FEELINGS

To identify your feelings, ask yourself the following:

- What am I feeling (e.g., sad, confused, frustrated)?
- What triggered the feeling (e.g., conversation with my boss, meeting, co-worker interaction)?
- Why did the trigger(s) cause this feeling?
- Where do I feel the feeling in my body (e.g., head, chest, stomach)?

To respond to your feelings, ask yourself the following:

- What does this feeling tell me about what I need or want?
- What is out of my control to meet my needs or wants?
- What is within my control to meet my needs or wants?

Process:

- To identify your feelings about a negative experience you had at work, reflect on and write your answers to each question in the first set of self-reflection prompts. (Note: Although the focus of this book is work, you can use the same steps for experiences outside of work.)
- To respond to your feelings, reflect on and write down your answers to the second set of self-reflection prompts.
- Ask yourself, what is the first step I can take to meet my needs or wants?
- Generate a list of one to three possible steps you can take to meet your needs or wants.
- Pick one step that you *can* do and *would* do to meet your needs or wants.
- This next step might seem simple but can be the hardest to do—take the step. Whatever that is. Do it.
- Practice, practice, practice! As with everything else you're learning, the steps will help you gain proficiency with the

skill. I am a fan of using nonwork experiences to gain practice with the skill, but you may have enough work hardship going on to provide you ample practice.

SEEK PROFESSIONAL COUNSELING

I believe that everybody needs and can benefit from counseling. It's not because I've been a counselor for over twenty years, or because I've trained and supervised other counselors. I am team counseling because I know what it's like to be a client. Having someone help me scratch some stuff out of my head is and has been a powerful experience. For me, having someone hold space and not judge me while I cried myself into exhaustion is invaluable. Having someone see behind my masks—my positions, my possessions, my performances—to see that I was just Tammy, a Black woman in the world who was just as afraid as I was courageous, who was just as unsure as I was confident, who needed help just as much as I helped others, who ultimately wants to please God so in the end I can hear him say, "Job well done, my good and faithful servant."

You're probably team counseling too. I hope that you have experienced the powerful and transformative nature of a professional counseling relationship or know someone who has. Perhaps you may already know where to find a counselor, what to look for in a counselor, and how to communicate your needs in a counseling relationship. If that is you, the following sections will be an affirmation and confirmation of what you already know.

But perhaps you are not team counseling. Maybe you are unsure of what professional counseling is or whether it can help *you*. Affordability might also be an issue, as is the case for many Black women seeking counseling. Costs for counseling services is a barrier for those who may not have health insurance and have to pay out of pocket. If this is you, the good news is that there may be low-cost options through community-based agencies and university-based settings or on a sliding fee scale through many private practitioners. However, accessibility to counseling services is an entirely different matter altogether.

Many of my clients have expressed their excitement about *finally* finding a Black female therapist who they didn't have to first explain their experience of being Black and female to before they could get to the primary reason for seeking counseling. For many Black women, having shared identity as Black women creates a level of safety and trust for clients to do the work of growth, healing, and change. And yet, accessibility is also about scheduling. The majority of my clients are professional Black women who can schedule a session on their lunch break or in the middle of the day, or who have access to environments conducive to teletherapy (video or phone sessions). However, an overwhelming majority of Black women, because of inflexible work schedules, caregiving responsibilities, or transportation, are not able to access counseling services. If you are one of those clients, seeking out counseling providers who offer early morning, evening, or night sessions through convenient formats such as teletherapy is a viable option. But affordability or accessibility may not be your reasons for not seeking counseling.

Perhaps you think counseling is for people who are "crazy," mentally ill, or "weak-minded," or who have *real* problems. I get it—stigma and lack of understanding about mental health as existing on a continuum that ranges from healthy and adaptive coping with life's challenges to severe impairment in coping has led to a commonly held belief (and myth) that counseling is for certain people with certain issues. The truth is that is simply untrue. Counseling is for *anyone* to talk about *anything*. You don't have to have something *wrong* with you or your life to seek counseling. You can seek counseling if you simply need to talk with a professional who will give you objective, unbiased insights about whatever the issue is. I mean, what other relationship do you have where, for one hour, the talk is all about you? Let me guess—none!

Of course, there might be entirely different reasons altogether. It could be you believe you can choose prayer or counseling but not both. Maybe you've tried to manage on your own and recognize that you need a professional counselor but don't know the steps to take to find one. If any of these sound familiar, the remaining sections in this chapter will provide you with the answers you need to get the help you deserve.

The American Counseling Association defines professional counseling as "a professional relationship that empowers diverse individuals, families, and groups to accomplish mental health, wellness, education, and career goals."[1] We see first and foremost that professional counseling is a professional relationship. The professional in this relationship has met minimum standards for education, training, supervised practice, and licensing. Therefore, conversations with your counselor shouldn't feel like conversations with one of your girlfriends (although at times they may). Further, a professional counseling relationship is one of empowerment that is meant to build you up, not break you down. Professional counselors also address issues that affect diverse client populations, and have an ethical mandate to center the social, cultural, and political realities of their clients throughout the therapeutic process. Therefore, it is reasonable to expect that your counselor has a basic understanding of how being Black and female may be affecting your experiences at work (and beyond) and thus incorporate counseling techniques that reflect that understanding. Finally, professional counseling addresses not only mental health and well-being but also issues related to education and work. If you need to talk about that boss who is making your work environment toxic, a professional counselor can handle that.

A professional counseling relationship is one of empowerment that is meant to build you up, not break you down.

Know that all professional counselors are not created equal. Professional counselors fall under a broad category of mental health professionals that includes a range of professions, each with a different scope of practice, research, ethical codes, training, and state licensing requirements, among other things. Therefore, knowing the different types of mental health professionals can help you feel better prepared to identify the right type of help. The list below is not exhaustive but is intended to give you a general idea of the different types of mental health professionals that exist. Again, you may be familiar with these distinctions, but, as you walk through your healing journey, spend some time with them to help you make the best decision for your mental health. Before we dig into the types of practitioners, it's a good idea to first establish what your unique needs are. Doing so will help you choose the best person to work with.

Know What You Need Help With

Let's take a step back. Before finding a counselor, think about what you want and need from them. First, consider your immediate issues. These can be family (relationship conflict, separation, divorce, trauma, problems with a child), personal (depression, anxiety, or trauma), or work based (conflicts with co-workers or supervisors, problems at work spilling over into your personal life). Take a few moments to write your needs here:

Sometimes counseling alone is not enough to address your mental health needs. For some, counseling and psychotropic medication can be a powerful therapeutic combination to treat mental health conditions such as depression, bipolar disorder, or anxiety. However, because of stigma and lack of awareness about the importance and occasional necessity for psychotropic medications to address mental health conditions, there might be a hesitancy to go the medication route.

I've had to work through this in sessions with clients where it became clear that medication might be indicated to help the client achieve the desired mental health outcomes that counseling alone was unable to achieve. Those conversations have often been in response to concerns that their conditions were not "serious enough" for medication, or fear that others would somehow know that they were taking medication, or that they didn't want to be dependent on medication. Maybe you've had some of these same concerns. What I tell my clients and what I will tell you is that your feelings and concerns are valid; however, taking medication can be a powerful tool in your toolbox for achieving mental and emotional stability.

I often stress that unless there is a reason why you would *need* to tell your friends you've started taking psychotropic medication, there is no reason they would *need* to know or *would* know. Unless of course they noticed positive changes in your mood and affect and you just felt the need to say, "Yeah, girl, this medication helps me get my mind right!" Otherwise, it ain't their business.

If the concern is about the medication itself, then know that it is perfectly okay and strongly encouraged to address your concerns about medication dependence, anticipated side effects, or any other concerns at the medication evaluation visit. As a patient, you have a right to ask questions and be informed about your mental health care. Thus, addressing these concerns with your counselor can not only reduce the stigma but also help you become a better advocate for your mental health.

You might be asking, "How do I know if I need medication?" Well, there are a number of factors that might suggest the need for a psychiatric evaluation for medication; however, the decision to be evaluated is not one you have to make alone. If you are already working with a professional counselor, the counselor might recommend a medication evaluation if you sought counseling, say, for depression, but there is minimal or no progress, or the depressive symptoms increase following a clinically significant period of counseling treatment. Scope of practice is also a factor. If you decide that you need medication and are not working with a counselor and choose to see a psychiatrist instead, you will likely be prescribed medication. Psychiatrists are medical doctors who operate from a medical/disease model.

So their first line of medical intervention will be medication and not counseling, because the latter is not their scope of practice. I've had to explain to those clients who lamented that psychiatrists just want to give 'em a pill (as opposed to counseling) that the psychiatrist was acting within the scope of their practice.

Regardless of where you stand on the issue of medication, I want you to hear it from me—needing and taking medication does not mean that something is wrong with you or that your worth decreases should you need to take it. Look at medication as another tool in your toolbox to help you be well and flourish. Take a moment to write your feelings about this:

_____

_____

_____

_____

_____

Keep in mind, you don't have to have your clinical needs completely figured out to find a professional counselor. Counselors don't expect that you will come to them super clear about the issue and the goals you want to achieve. An effective counselor will help you sift through the confusion and chaos, gain clarity on what the issue is, and identify how best they can help you. In the following sections, we'll dig into the different types of mental health professionals available.

Counselors and Therapists[2]

Professional counselors are master's-level trained professionals with a degree in a mental health–related field (e.g., an MA or MS in counseling). Professional counselors can diagnose mental health conditions and provide individual, family, couples/marriage, and group counseling for a range of clinical issues. Licensure examples include (these vary by state):

- Licensed Professional Counselor (LPC)
- Licensed Marriage and Family Therapist (LMFT)
- Licensed Clinical Alcohol and Drug Abuse Counselor (LCADC)

Clinical social workers are master's-level trained professionals with a master's degree in social work (MSW). Clinical social workers can diagnose mental health conditions and provide individual, family, couples/marriage, and group counseling for a range of clinical issues. Clinical social workers are also trained in case management and systems advocacy. Licensure examples include (they vary by state):

- Licensed Clinical Social Worker (LCSW)
- Licensed Independent Clinical Social Worker (LICSW)

Psychologists are doctoral-level trained professionals (with a PhD or PsyD) with specialties in clinical, counseling, or school psychology. Psychologists can diagnose mental health conditions and provide individual, family, couples/marriage, and group counseling for a range of clinical issues. Psychologists may also conduct assessments, evaluations, and psychological testing. Psychology is the profession most people associate with counseling but, as illustrated here, there are other professions out there providing counseling. Licensure varies by state.

Specialists Who Prescribe and Manage Medication

Psychiatrists are medical doctors (MDs) who have completed medical and psychiatry training. Psychiatrists can diagnose, prescribe, and manage medication for mental health conditions. Some provide therapy; however, their primary scope is prescribing and managing medication. Psychiatrists sometimes work in conjunction with professional counselors and clinical social workers when medication and counseling are clinically appropriate. Licensure:

• Licensed as an MD in the state where they practice.

Psychiatric or mental health nurse practitioners are master's-level or doctoral-level (with an MS or PhD) trained nursing professionals who specialize in mental health diagnoses. They can diagnose, provide counseling, and prescribe and manage medication, although the ability to do the latter varies by state. Some states require that they are supervised by a licensed psychiatrist. Licensure:

- Licensed as a nurse in the state where they practice.

In highlighting these different types of mental health professionals, my hope is to illuminate that the therapeutic approach and professional relationship will vary based on many of these factors. But knowing the differences can also help you know what to look for when you're ready to search.

FINDING AND WORKING WITH A COUNSELOR

So you have pinpointed your needs, and you have an understanding of who to look for. Now, how do you go about locating the right counselor, and how do you discern whether someone is going to be a good fit? Finding a professional counselor can seem daunting, but it doesn't have to be. A good place to start is within your personal network. The best referral can be from someone you know and trust—a family member, a friend, a colleague. In fact, roughly 80 percent of my client referrals come from current or past clients. A friend or family member told them how helpful I was for them—*ahem*—and they wanted to see for themselves. Still, approach it with open eyes. The counselor who was a good fit for your family member or friend may not be right for you. What you need from the counseling relationship may be completely different than your referral source. But knowing people who are getting professional help and benefiting from it can be just the encouragement you need to take that step.

Other referrals may come from your primary care physician or ob-gyn. There is growing recognition among health care professionals for the need to take an integrated approach to wellness because mental health and physical health are interrelated. Therefore, you can consult with your physicians to help you identify mental health professionals who may be in their network. If you are looking for therapy, ask specifically for that type of referral, because physicians can be quick to give you a prescription for antidepressants and call it a day. Mental health treatment is not the scope of practice of a primary care physician or ob-gyn, so be clear when you ask for a referral to a mental health professional. If your physician does refer you to someone, expect that you may be asked to give written authorization to both parties to exchange information to coordinate care. Coordinated care is ideal and a best practice.

If you're not comfortable asking for a referral from friends and family or your physicians, research is also a strong option. If mental health (or behavioral health) counseling is a benefit of your health insurance, you can request (or view online) a directory of in-network mental health providers in your area who take your insurance. Searching by in-network providers can take the guesswork and frustration out of finally finding a counselor only to call and hear, "Sorry, we don't take your insurance." You should also inquire about any out-of-pocket expenses (e.g., co-pays, co-insurance, deductibles) and whether the provider will handle the billing (which is customary but not always). Something that is not always known or shared by the counselor is that in order to bill your health insurance for services, the counselor will have to render a mental health diagnosis to receive payment from your insurance, and that diagnosis becomes a part of your medical record. The process works the same when you see a physician. The physician renders a medical diagnosis and files an insurance claim to receive the portion of the payment that the insurance company is responsible for. A mental health diagnosis may be a nonissue for most, but if for example you are in the military, a diagnosis may bring stigma and certain restrictions in duties.

There are also a number of free online directories for counselors and therapists. Directories are an effective tool for finding a professional counselor because of the range of available information you can use to search. Generally, you can see photos and profiles, specializations, fee and insurance information, and so on. There are several directories specific to Black women (e.g., Therapy for Black Girls and Black Female Therapists) or Black, Indigenous, and People of Color (BIPOC) (e.g., Boris Lawrence Henson Foundation and Clinicians of Color). There are also directories at websites like *Psychology Today*, where you can search for counselors by race and gender, referral issue, and more. Looking through profile pages may seem like a daunting task, so the more you are able to refine your search, the more likely you will find the right fit for you. Which brings me to my next point—how do you know if the professional counselor is a good fit? The short answer: You don't always know—at least not right away.

How to Determine Fit

A professional counseling relationship is just like any other relationship in that what makes the relationship work is a mix of personality, mutual investment in the relationship, communication, and trust. Sometimes you have to "date" (figuratively, of course) a few therapists before you find the right one. Remember when I said it's important to know what you need help with and your goals for counseling? Well, both are critical for determining fit. At minimum, you want someone who can demonstrate competence and confidence to help you—and somebody you feel comfortable sharing your story with.

Start with the information you can find out about their skills and specialization. Do they say they work with Black women specifically? Do they work with the issue(s) you need help with? Does the profile or website speak to you in some way? I've had many self-referred clients say things to me like "It was something about your eyes" or "You look like you meant business" or simply "I chose you because you were a Black woman."

Another way to determine fit is through a consultation. Phone or video consultations are essentially a brief prescreening opportunity for both the counselor and client. For the counselor, a phone or video consultation helps to determine whether the client is a good fit based on referral issue and the counselor's scope of practice. For example, the counselor might ask what issue you are seeking help with and who referred you. They will likely provide some general information about their practice and how to begin counseling services with them.

For the client, a phone or video consultation can help you get a feel for the counselor's personality and approach. The consultation is an important opportunity to ask questions that may be important to determine fit. For example, if you haven't previously determined it, ask, "Have you ever worked with Black women clients?" "Have you worked with ___ issue?" Once all questions and concerns have been addressed, and if it seems like a mutual fit, the counselor will likely want to schedule you for a first session.

What to Expect at the First Session

Your first, or intake, session is an information-gathering session for the counselor. The format of the intake session may be structured or semi-structured. A structured intake session is usually guided by the use of some type of assessment, testing, or diagnostic technique to gather relevant background information. A semi-structured intake session may include a mix of the above with interview-style questions. The time frame for an intake session time can range anywhere from fifty to ninety minutes. The goal is to gather enough information to determine what your main areas of focus will be and how best to approach them. By the end, you should have a reasonable understanding of the counselor's clinical impressions and recommendations for counseling. If there is mutual agreement to work together, there should be some discussion about next steps. If not, the counselor can make some recommendations for how to find someone else to work with. Again, intake session activities will vary, but this is what you should be able to reasonably expect from the first session. You should also have a sense of whether this is someone you want to work with.

Just like the phone or video consultation, the intake provides another connection point to determine whether the professional counselor is a good fit. It is okay to ask questions about their counseling framework and how that framework will guide the clinical process. It's also okay to share your comments or concerns about the process. If you had a previous positive experience with a counselor or an approach that worked for you, share that. Conversely, if you had negative experiences with counseling, share those too. A positive counselor response to your concerns is a good sign that they will be responsive down the line. A negative, dismissive response is a sign not to come back. The onus of making the experience a positive one is on the professional. Saying whether something works or doesn't work for you is on you. Once the intake session is complete, ask yourself: "How did the counselor make me feel? Did I feel heard? Did I feel understood? Am I satisfied with how my questions were answered? Was the counselor empathic? Was he, she, or they engaging or distant? Is the path forward clear?" The answers to these questions are basics of fit. If you don't feel seen, heard, and valued at the outset, it's not a good fit.

It is important to note that the intake session is unique in that it is diagnostic in nature, so the types of questions and interactions that happen there may look quite different from subsequent sessions. The counselor who is focused on getting questions answered in the intake session may be less so in subsequent sessions as the nature of the therapeutic relationship changes over time. So, unless something happens in the intake session to scare you off, like the counselor talks more about their issues than yours (this actually happened to me—I ran fast!), says or does something offensive, or just does not give off good vibes or energy, a good rule of thumb is three sessions for a trial period. If you are able to establish a good rhythm and relationship with the counselor after three sessions, that is a sign that it may be a good fit. If not, it may be a sign to move on.

HELPFUL TIPS

- It's okay to not be okay. But it's also okay to get help.
- Finding the right counselor for you is a process. The tools provided here are meant to be a guide. The best tool you have is your gut. Listen to it.
- If at first you don't succeed, try again. Protecting your peace is worth your investment of time and energy.

Chapter 6

HAVE 20/20 VISION

The year 2020 was supposed to be the year of vision. Do you remember all the excitement and optimism you felt at the start of that year? Like many, I, too, believed that the year would be special. Change was in the air. To acknowledge that sense of change, on January 1 I did a new thing: I made a vision board. If the year was going to be special and if I expected something different, then I needed to do something different.

I was proud of my board. It was all the things that vision boards, I suspected, were made of. On the one hand was the actual stuff—things that reflect who I am now and how I move in the world—love of God, family, and the importance of self-care. On the other hand was the aspirational stuff—my goal to become a writer as well as images and names of folks whom I admire and want to meet someday, like forever first lady Michelle Obama, Oprah, and Mary J. Blige. And, of

course, I topped it all off with a healthy sprinkle of empowerment, with quotes like "She's going to make it after all!" and
"Women rule the world!" Yes! My board reflected where I was
but also where I believed I and other women were headed—to
the top!

And then the COVID-19 pandemic hit. And just like that,
my optimism was replaced with fear, worry, and uncertainty:
How long will this last? When will we get back to normal
again? Why can't I find toilet tissue in the store? You know—
serious questions. As the year unfolded with the pandemic
and civil unrest following the murders of Breonna Taylor and
George Floyd, something shifted in me. I started to take a hard
look at the vision board that by now had somehow fallen behind
some shoeboxes next to my bed. I started to reassess my perspective. The question of "Why is this happening?" was turning
into "Why is this happening *for* me?" What if, I wondered, this
moment was exactly what I needed to get my mind right? What
if the pandemic was really a pause, an opportunity, or even a
gift? Maybe this was the transformation that others felt but certainly couldn't have predicted.

With the perspective shift, the things on my vision board
were sharpening into focus. I could see that my faith was growing stronger. I was spending more time at home with my family.
I was reading and resting more. I could no longer use "I don't
have time" as an excuse to avoid writing. As it turned out, 2020
hadn't stopped my visions from manifesting at all. What became

crystal clear was the importance of having vision and keeping it in front of you—literally. The vision board that had begun to collect dust was resurrected and tacked to the wall next to my bed. At the beginning of each day, I woke up with my vision in front of me. My vision board anchored me on those particularly tough days when optimism fatigue set in and staying positive was overwhelming. My vision board also helped me to see the necessity of having 20/20 vision as a tool, particularly for Black women, to thrive at work despite experiences of race and gender stereotypes that dehumanize and devalue our work and our worth.

So, you might be asking yourself: "What is 20/20 vision? And why is it important for me to have?"

WHAT IS 20/20 VISION?

In brief, 20/20 vision means *having clarity about who you are and showing up as that person authentically and unapologetically.* Twenty-twenty vision is rooted in both your ability to see and know yourself and your worth, *as well as* maintaining your awareness of the stereotypes that exist about Black women that limit the way others may see you. For us, having 20/20 vision is essential to our ability to navigate work—and ultimately life.

Because cultural messaging perpetuates race and gender stereotypes that distort the true reality of Black women's lived experiences, that messaging also forces us to live in a state of what I call the *matrix of visibility*: the range of behaviors that Black women engage in to control how we are perceived. When we censor or silence our voices to make others see us as agreeable and not aggressive, we're matrixing. When we dress or wear our hair a certain way so that we can be seen as professional according to white standards, we are matrixing. This matrixing is additional labor that, over time, comes with a physical and emotional tax that costs more than it benefits. Therefore, having clarity about who you are regardless of how others see you allows you to be upright in an environment that tells you that bending over is your only rightful position. When you have 20/20 vision, you can move onward and forward knowing that showing up as you are is indeed enough. Period.

Why Having 20/20 Vision Is Important

For the clients in my private practice, the consequences of not having clear vision are damaging. Ninety-five percent of my clients are Black women from various professional backgrounds. And, while many of them do not initially seek counseling for work-related issues, I often later assess that work-related stress is an underlying factor of, if not a major contributor to, why they are seeking counseling. Because many of my clients are in high-status positions, or are "the only" (or one of few) Black women in their positions, we spend many counseling sessions processing the extra weight and pressure from expectations, real or perceived, to be the exemplar representative for all Black women.

One client in particular, a Black female professional who sought counseling for depression and anxiety, disclosed that as the only Black woman in a predominantly white office setting, she experienced racist comments from co-workers and was overlooked for job opportunities despite being highly qualified. Yet she remained mostly silent on these issues at work for fear of being seen as the "angry Black woman." But the pattern of silencing herself, I assessed, started much earlier in life with familial and spiritual messages about silence as respectable, Christian, ladylike behavior. It made sense, then, that in my initial assessment I determined a toxic work environment was the underlying cause of the client's depressive and anxiety symptoms.

My client had realized that this messaging was no longer serving her, if it ever did. In light of that, my work with her was deeper than just facilitating coping skills for work. Rather, it was also about creating a safe space for this Black woman to find her voice and learn how to use it. And here is where our real challenge came: clarifying a vision to guide and ground her voice. For everyone, but particularly for long-silenced Black women, there is no voice without clear vision.

It's important to note here that whenever I work with Black women dealing with work-related stress, the beginning stages of our clinical work involve psychoeducation about the effects of race and gender stereotypes on their work experiences. Providing psychoeducation helps to normalize my clients' experiences by highlighting that what happened to them has also happened to other Black women. You know what I am talking about if you ever had a situation happen at work and you asked yourself questions like "Am I overreacting?" "Maybe I am being too emotional about this?" Further, psychoeducation about race and gender stereotypes also helps to bring clarity to their experiences so that as therapy progresses, they will feel empowered to explore and then engage in healthy and helpful coping skills.

After the initial stages of our work together, the client gained valuable insights about the impact of stereotypes on her work situation, which empowered her to advocate for herself on the job. Being clear about who she was, her beliefs, and her values helped her be content with her decision to remain in her current job despite the fact that nothing around her had changed. While we had spent considerable time in previous sessions discussing the health implications of remaining in a toxic work environment, ethically I had to respect my client's decision to do what she felt was best—even if it was not clinically recommended. Thus, even though I had provided my client psychoeducation about the impact of race and gender stereotypes on mental and physical health, my client decided that maintaining her job was more important than prioritizing her health. She decided to do what many of us do in these situations: sacrifice our health to pay our bills and take care of our families. Yet, over time it was evident that my client became more comfortable with advocating for herself and felt good about the improvements in her mood and anxiety, which she attributed to her new coping skills. All seemed to be going well—until one day she showed up for our session in tears.

She shared that she was diagnosed as prediabetic at a recent doctor's visit. My client acknowledged that she had some biological predisposition to diabetes; however, she was emphatic that work stress was to blame for this new medical condition. And she was devastated. She expressed sadness and guilt about her diagnosis, which I normalized given the context. I normalized the anger she felt because she "prioritized" a job over on her own health and well-being. Anger that she had "let it get that bad." Anger that she felt "stuck" because she needed her job. Her feelings represented the range that many of us experience while trying to navigate unhealthy work environments because we need our jobs. For most of us, work is a necessity, not a choice.

Yet, while these negative work experiences might be necessary for maintaining our households, they are not good for maintaining our health. Twenty-twenty vision allows you to navigate these situations with clarity about who you are and empower yourself to make healthy decisions that prioritize your wellness. For Black women, the notion of us putting our well-being first sounds revolutionary, right? It would seem that way when all you've ever been told is that being Mammy is the righteous thing to be. But I've slid off the therapist couch to tell you that Mammy is dead. Stress killed her.

As a general principle, I believe that having 20/20 vision begins and ends with asking and seeking answers to important yet often unexplored existential questions. For you to have any level of clarity about who you are and then audaciously show up authentically and unapologetically as that person, you must ask yourself: (a) "Who am I?" (b) "What do I believe?" (c) "What do I value?" These are essential questions, and also big questions—let's be honest, most of us are not sitting around thinking about our thinking. Yet, if someone asked you any or all of the above questions, could you answer them with confidence?

Having 20/20 vision begins and ends with asking and seeking answers to important yet often unexplored existential questions.

If you are to obtain any level of well-being at work, it is essential to examine your sense of who you are, what you believe, and what you value. However, let me be clear: Asking and seeking answers to these questions is—like wellness—a journey rather than a destination. Each age and stage of life offers us an opportunity to deepen our understanding of ourselves. And like any journey, we should enjoy the view. For Black women in particular, our view is often obstructed by harmful messaging that distorts how others see us as well as how we see ourselves. What we need is corrective vision through which we can deconstruct this harmful messaging and then reconstruct new messaging that allows us to be who we say we are.

SELF-REFLECTION

As we begin to deconstruct this harmful messaging and develop corrective vision, we can engage in the process of self-reflection. This method, which includes self-examination and self-exploration, leads us to greater awareness and positive behavioral change. As we discussed previously, being clear on who you are, your beliefs, and your values helps you avoid internalizing the harmful and contradictory messages you receive at work.

In my private practice, I have observed numerous benefits of self-reflection. For example, facilitating self-reflection with clients who are navigating work-related stress led them to report increased clarity, self-advocacy, self-empowerment, well-being, job satisfaction, productivity, and healthy boundaries. For some, self-reflection also led to employment or career changes. Having clarity about who you are and what your beliefs and values are lets you develop self-governing principles that become your personal compass for navigating work roles and relationships. This personal compass can also guide decisions about where you work. Let's face it, one of the worst things that can happen is going to work for a company whose mission and values in principle sounded really good—only to start working there and find that they were good in word but not in deed. And worse yet, as an employee, you're now expected to be complicit in their misdeeds. Maintaining this type of clarity can provide a helpful and healthy guide that sets you up for future professional success. To that end, the following sections will provide three self-reflection activities that include reflection prompts, steps, and tips to help you independently explore your sense of who you are, your beliefs, and your values.

SELF-REFLECTION EXERCISE

Prompt #1 Who am I?

- What three words describe the essence of who I am (e.g., authentic, fair, truth seeker)?
- I am my most authentic self when I _____ (e.g., when I take care of myself, when I am doing what I love).
- Is my authentic self evident in how I show up at work?
- What barriers stop me from showing up authentically at work?
- Who do I want to become (think characteristic ["I want to become more authentic"], a state of being ["I want to

have more joy in my life"], or a vocation [I want to be a best-selling author"])?

- Am I on the path toward who I want to become (what evidence do you or others see that signifies you are on the right track to becoming who you want to become)?

Prompt #2: What do I believe?

- What family messages have shaped my beliefs about work?
- What societal messages have shaped my beliefs about work?
- What are my beliefs about myself in relationship to work?
- Which identities influence how I navigate work (e.g., race, gender, spirituality, sexual orientation)?
- How do my beliefs help me at work?
- How do my beliefs hinder me at work?

Prompt #3: What do I value?

- What values are most important to me (e.g., self-care, justice, service)?
- What values are least important to me (e.g., fame, popularity, risk)?
- How have my values changed over time?

- What do I value in a work environment (e.g., trust, transparency, support)?
- What makes me feel valued at work (e.g., respect, support, transparency)?
- Do the values of my current employer reflect my values? If not, how are they different?

Process:

- Choose a method to record your reflections. Record your reflections in a journal or with a note-taking app on your phone. You can keep it simple and use an inexpensive journal or notebook, or get creative (e.g., colored pens or pencils, markers, stickers). For some, it is easier to verbalize their thoughts out loud as opposed to writing them down, so audio or video recording can also be a great option.
- Pick the time of day that you are the most reflective. This can be at the start or end of your day, but it should be a time when you have minimal distractions. It does not matter when you do it, only that you do it consistently. Make an appointment with yourself by putting it in your calendar, and stick to it.
- Create a reflective environment. Minimize distractions to allow your thoughts to flow. Practice deep breathing (i.e., inhaling for four counts and exhaling for five

counts), meditation, or mindfulness. Adding soft music and pleasant scents can also be helpful in getting you in the reflective zone.

- Freestyle it! Using the self-reflection prompts, record everything that comes to your mind without judgment. Don't set any expectations for how much you should write or speak. It is okay if you come up with only a few words, sentences, or images. You will have multiple opportunities to get something down. Try not to get frustrated with the process. These are big questions that may not have immediate or obvious answers. Tell yourself, "I am worth investing in this process."

- Review, revise, and reconstruct as necessary. Reviewing what you have written serves as a reminder for your journey and can also be a catalyst for deeper reflection. As the breadth and depth of your reflections occur, replace any inaccurate, unhelpful, and unhealthy thoughts with accurate, helpful, and healthy thoughts that empower you. For example, "I'm a failure because I haven't achieved what others my age have achieved" could be replaced with "I do not have to compete with anyone else" or "I am capable of creating the life I want." Reviewing, revising, and reconstructing leads to positive self-affirmations that can empower and motivate you to move onward and forward authentically and unapologetically!

- Keep your vision of yourself in front of you. Post-it notes are an inexpensive and easily accessible tool for keeping your vision in front of you and giving yourself a daily deposit of positivity. Create positive self-affirmation notes that begin with "I AM..." and post them at work, home, and even your car. Every day I tell myself: "I AM a teacher. I AM wise. I AM abundant. I AM great. I AM God's excellence. I AM worthy. I AM enough. I AM free." These words are my daily love notes to myself that remind me of who I am. At work, place your positive self-affirmation notes on your desk, computer, wall, cubicle, in your phone—anywhere that is visible but also accessible. At home, place your notes on your mirrors around your house. Keeping your vision of who you are in front of you armors you so that when the darts are thrown your way, they may prick you (because you are not a superwoman) but they won't penetrate.

HELPFUL TIPS

- Be realistic. Set an achievable time frame for your self-reflection activities. I recommend working on them at least once each day for seven days to start.
- Be consistent. It doesn't matter when you do your self-reflection, but make a habit to do it at least once a day.

- Be open. Self-reflection helps you go deeper. Be open to what you find beneath the surface. All of those pieces are a part of you—but you define you.
- Be kind to yourself. It's okay if it's hard in the beginning. Remember, most of us are not thinking about our thinking, so consider this process as building a new muscle. It takes time. The idea here is proficiency over perfection. Have some grace for your pace!

Chapter 7

"NO." IS A COMPLETE SENTENCE

The year 2021 was the year of "No" for Black women. When Pulitzer Prize–winning journalist and MacArthur Fellow Nikole Hannah-Jones refused tenure at the University of North Carolina at Chapel Hill in July 2021 after she was initially denied but then accepted a tenured chair position at Howard University, Black women everywhere were like, "Sis did that!" When US Open and Australian Open tennis champion Naomi Osaka withdrew from the 2021 French Open and Wimbledon to prioritize her mental health, Black women everywhere were like, "That's right! Take care of your mental health!" And when USA Gymnastics Olympic medalist Simone Biles withdrew from the 2021 Olympic team finals and the all-around competition to take care of her mental health, Black women everywhere were in agreement that "*y'all* not about to stress us out!" They—we—understood the assignment: Self-care is the most important job you will ever have. And to be effective at that job, you must set boundaries.

Like "self-care" and "wellness," "boundaries" has become a buzzword that has gained popularity over the last few years. But most people didn't grow up learning what boundaries are, why they're important, or how to set them. This is particularly true of Black women. In the following sections, I will define and discuss the importance of personal and professional boundaries and some of the challenges that Black women have with setting them, and offer steps and helpful tips to set boundaries with confidence.

BOUNDARIES DEFINED

When I talk about boundaries, what I mean are the personal and professional limits we set around what we access and what or who has access to us. As a form of self-care, boundaries are protective and selective in that they are the metaphorical lines you draw in the sand to protect your mind, body, and spirit. On the one hand, boundaries are what you access. When you give your attention, time, or energy to certain people, places, and things and not others, you are setting a boundary. On the other hand, boundaries are also the access others have to you, both personally and professionally.

Personal Boundaries

Personal boundaries encompass emotional and physical boundaries. When we set emotional boundaries, we are exercising our ability to recognize, respond to, and express feelings in a manner that helps us feel in control. Have you ever been mad at yourself because somebody or something *made* you feel some kind of way? Or you let somebody get under your skin? Your response in those situations is likely due to a lack of emotional boundaries. When you lack emotional boundaries, others can easily control how you feel, unintentionally or very intentionally. Conversely, when you possess strong emotional boundaries, you can feel more in control of your feelings and how you express them.

Emotional boundaries also help you to avoid taking on others' feelings. Do you have that friend or family member who always calls with bad news and by the end of the conversation you feel emotionally drained? I think we all know people who make you their emotional dumping ground. Setting an emotional boundary in this scenario might mean not answering the call or answering it and setting limits for what you can and will discuss (e.g., "That sounds really important but I cannot discuss that right now. Is there someone else you can talk to about this?"). Sound easier said than done? You are right.

Setting boundaries with others can make us feel guilty that we're not being a good friend, partner, employee, etc.—you have probably experienced this in very real ways. If you have been previously loose with your boundaries, those around you may not be accustomed to you having boundaries. So guess what? You will certainly encounter resistance when you set a boundary. But *your* boundaries are for *you*. This is an important point to remember because emotional boundaries help you to take care of your emotional needs and feel more in control. Being clear that your boundaries are for you is also important because you can expect that repeat boundary violations will happen. Being rooted in your belief that your boundaries matter can help you persist in setting and then resetting boundaries with people who intentionally and unintentionally bypass them.

My clients often talk about feeling exhausted when having to reset boundaries with the same folks and question whether it's worth it for them to do so. My response to them and my message to you is I don't get to decide for you whether you believe you deserve to have boundaries and thus the right to set and reset them. That is a personal decision. But what I will say is it's worth it to ask yourself if you can live with (because living with it unfortunately is a default for many of us) and thrive in a relationship where your boundaries are repeatedly ignored. If the answer is yes, what does that say about you and your worth?

Physical boundaries are exactly that—this is the control of the physical access others have to you. Specifically, it means access to your physical space (such as house, office, etc.) but also your physical body (personal space). The type of relationship (e.g., family, friends, co-workers), the distance within the relationship (e.g., personal versus professional), and the dynamics in the relationship (e.g., trust versus mistrust, harmonious versus conflicted) should determine how much physical access others have to you and how flexible or inflexible you are with that access. Access is key here because boundaries are like keys to your home. Of course, only a select few should have keys to your house.

Think of physical boundaries as concentric circles. You exist at the center of these circles. The circles closest to the center represent the relationships closest to you (partner or spouse, children, family, friends)—your inner circle, if you will. Assuming that there is closeness, trust, and harmony with those in your inner circle, your boundaries are likely to be more flexible (i.e., greater access to you). For example, a partner or spouse will have more access to your physical space and body than your non-intimate relationships.

Further, you are also likely to be more inflexible with your physical boundaries with those relationships that exist in the outer circles (e.g., professional, community, society). For example, you might be more inclined to set a physical boundary with a co-worker who walks up and touches your hair versus your girlfriend who does the same as an affectionate gesture. Relatedly, professional boundaries, like personal boundaries, are equally important if you are to be well *and* excel at work.

Professional Boundaries

Professional boundaries are effectively about roles, responsibilities, and relationships. Being clear about your role and the job you were hired to do is an important aspect of professional boundaries. One of the main sources of stress and discontent I hear from clients is being made to wear too many hats at work, an experience also expressed by my research participants. In fact, feeling overworked is one of the top complaints I hear about work. I am sure you don't have to think hard or long about whether you've personally experienced being overworked, but I want you to reflect on a time when wearing too many hats was your experience at work. How did that experience affect you personally and professionally? My hope for you is that you gain a greater sense of clarity as you are prompted to reflect on your experiences throughout the book. Through reflecting on where you've been, you can think about where you want to go. But more importantly, reflection helps us to break our unhealthy tendency as Black women to overlook or minimize the impact that these experiences have on us *because* we are Black women.

As a group, the mental and physical ramifications of being overworked are a part of our historical and collective experience as Black women, along with the internalized messaging that we should be working hard. Not only hard—but twice as hard. As we've already discussed, when we internalize these messages, we believe that performing multiples roles is what we should do. And we feel guilty when we don't.

Clarity and certainty about your role and responsibilities at work are essential to having healthy professional boundaries and relationships. Particularly, performing the primary role and responsibilities for which you were hired and are being paid for. Here, it's necessary for me to reiterate the impact of slavery and race and gender stereotypes to this discussion. Enslaved Black women and girls simultaneously occupied roles and relationships as work mules, mammies, and surrogate mamas.

Clarity and certainty about your role and responsibilities at work are essential to having healthy professional boundaries and relationships.

An image of a Black woman nursing a Black baby on one breast and a white baby on the other comes to mind. That image conjures up so many feelings in me—sadness, anger, rage, disgust, empathy—and curiosity. As I study that image, I wonder what it must have been like to be the woman in that picture. I wonder what her relationship was to her body—a body that was used and abused. I wonder what she felt when she looked down at the slaveholder's child feeding on milk that was meant for her own baby.

Metaphorically, Black women must still deal with others suckling at our breasts. We are still expected to nurture and caretake at work, at home, and in our communities. We are expected to make everybody feel good and uplifted. We are expected to be the trusted and loyal confidantes of our co-workers. We are expected to be "team players" who willingly and happily take on additional work responsibilities, often without compensation, with the expectation of being perfect in performing said responsibilities. And if we don't perform as expected, the consequences are often swift and painful. This additional labor costs us mentally, physically, and spiritually.

But let me be clear: Mammy is not your role. Others will try to convince you that it is. At times, you may even agree.

I am here to sound the alarm warning you that it is not your role. If you have been seeking permission to free yourself, here it is! Let me also stress that I am in no way advocating absolute rejection of nurturing or caretaking behaviors. It is absolutely okay and sometimes necessary to fulfill those roles. The important takeaway is that it is not okay to perform these roles because others expect you to. Performing the role and responsibilities for which you were hired is more than enough.

THE COST OF POOR BOUNDARIES

The impact of poor boundaries at work is evident with many of my Black female clients. I receive frequent reports of stress and burnout because they are overworked and underpaid. I've also observed that the stress and burnout are not always the fault of others in the workplace. Sometimes it's because of our own inaction. For some clients, they lack the skill to set boundaries at work. They don't know how to leave work at work, to ask for more money or help, or to confront the co-worker who offended them. Yet for others, the mere thought of setting boundaries provokes fear or guilt. And this fear and guilt are rooted in slavery and the resulting stereotypes.

The Origins of Our Guilt

The sexual and labor exploitation of Black women and girls during slavery are critical components to the lack of respect for

Black women's (and girls') boundaries. Black women's and girls' bodies were used for pleasure and profit without consent and protection of the law. During slave auctions, Black women and girls were forced to stand naked on auction blocks where white men and women "inspected" their bodies for fitness for work. For enslaved Black women and girls, "fitness" was determined by their ability to work as domestic and field slaves as well as bear children to become enslaved. Therefore, during these inspections, enslaved women and girls had physical examinations that involved things like having their breasts grabbed and every orifice of their bodies examined to determine childbearing ability. The part that makes me sick is that all of this happened in public spheres for public viewing, and it was perfectly legal!

Though slavery has ended, its effects continue to permeate every aspect of our daily lives, such that Black women and girls still have to fight to protect our humanity and who has access to it. However, because many of us have internalized the dehumanizing messages associated with race and gender stereotypes, restricting that access is difficult and seemingly impossible.

My clients frequently make statements like "I am afraid to set boundaries because I worry people will think I am an angry Black woman." Or "I feel guilty about saying no because I don't want to seem ungrateful." Or "I feel guilty for saying no because everybody expects me to say yes." Sound familiar? How many times have you restrained yourself from setting a boundary because you worried about how others would perceive you because you are a Black woman? I am sure you do not remember the exact moment you learned the message that saying no was not an option, but somewhere along the way I am sure you did. In many ways, many of us are raised with it; we internalize it. Thus, setting boundaries not only causes guilt, which is "I've done something bad," but worse, it also causes shame, which is "I am bad." Please believe— guilt and shame are a deadly combination. When we believe that setting limits on what we access and allow to access us is not only bad, but also that we are bad people for doing it, it leads to a vicious cycle that can kill us figuratively and literally.

Accept the Challenge

Make no mistake, setting boundaries is a challenge. As we learned, people will be unaccustomed to your boundaries, and, further, they benefit from your not having them. I'll say it again: Folks will resist your boundaries because they benefit from your not having them. The boss who gives you ten jobs even though your salary is for the one job you were hired to do benefits from your working twice as hard. To some employers, you may be considered cheap and frankly disposable labor. They don't have to pay you what you're worth because to the employer you have no worth (or very little), and if you don't like it (or they don't need you anymore), they can replace you. But if you buy into the message that you have to work twice as hard or play the game to prove your worth to people who aren't invested in your worth, you will lose. Yes, you might win in other ways—working twice as hard might get you the job, the promotion, or a pat on the back. But what did you lose along the way?

I want you to know that if you have learned to say yes, you can also learn to say no. Boundary setting is not genetic. It is a skill. And, like any skill, you can become proficient with practice. The following sections are designed to help you do just that: set boundaries with confidence and competence.

YOU'RE IN MY PERSONAL SPACE

Certain boundary violations (e.g., physical) will require that you set a boundary immediately. A personal example comes to mind. Earlier in my career, I worked as a residential counselor for adolescent boys. One day during a group counseling session, one of my clients got in my personal space and became verbally aggressive. The youth in the program had a history of trauma, mental health disorders, and behavioral disorders, so aggression toward staff was common. So, although I was not shocked when this particular client became aggressive, it was still necessary for me to set a clear boundary.

I looked the youth squarely in the eyes and said, "You need to back up right now and have a seat." He continued to threaten me and yell profanities. I took a deep breath and said, "You are violating my personal space. You need to back up and return to your seat." We had a stare-off for what seemed like forever—but guess what he did? He went and sat down.

This is an extreme example; my hope is that your physical boundaries are not being violated in this way, or worse. The takeaway here is that severity of the boundary violation may determine how a boundary gets communicated. We'll learn more about this in the following exercise.

BOUNDARY WORK

We begin by determining the type of boundary you need or want to set, and why you are setting it. This is an important first step to building and maintaining healthy boundaries. Being clear about the reason why you're setting a boundary helps to anchor you against the resistance you will encounter from others. Remember, your boundaries are for you, so if the other person doesn't benefit from it, you will get resistance. But you need to know and be okay with why the boundary needs to be set.

What Kind of Boundary Do You Need to Set?

First, determine whether you need to set personal boundaries (i.e., emotional, physical), professional boundaries (i.e., role clarification, time), or a combination of both. Some helpful questions to ask yourself:

- What is it that bothers me about this situation?
- Why am I feeling _____ (identify feeling), and who or what triggered these feelings?
- Next, ask yourself, what is the ultimate, best result of your setting this boundary?

Finally, consider the pros and cons of setting the boundary versus not setting the boundary. For example, how will setting the boundary help me (pro)? How will setting the boundary hurt me (con)? How will *not* setting the boundary help me (pro)? How will *not* setting this boundary hurt me (con)? If you were to work it out in your notebook, it might look like this:

Boundary I want to set: Not bringing work home
Desired outcome(s): Freeing up my time to do nonwork-related stuff; more rest and relaxation

Pros	Cons
Increased free time at nights and weekends	Work piling up
More time with my loved ones	Missed deadlines
More time to relax and unwind	Less time to socialize at work
More sleep	Waking up earlier to do work
Less stress and burnout	

———

Take a moment to consider your own scenario. Got it? Great! Next, you must determine the most effective way to communicate the boundary. Is it written (via email, text, letter)? Is it oral (a lunch meeting, over the phone, or video)? Is it nonverbal (taking breaks/lunches/vacation, leaving work at work, making appointments with yourself)? There are several factors to consider in determining the mode of communicating a boundary: timing and comfort level. Let's look at each in turn.

Timing and Comfort Level

With regard to timing, I recommend setting the boundary as close to the boundary violation as possible—this is often most beneficial for you and your desired outcome. Depending on the type of boundary violation, the need to set the boundary may be immediate. However, most of the time it is okay and advisable to give yourself a day or two to regroup before you respond. My general recommendation is to set the boundary within twenty-four to forty-eight hours.

There is good reason for this: How much time and energy have you lost thinking about something somebody did that bothered you before you actually addressed the situation? I have lost hours, days, weeks replaying a situation in my mind that I needed to address but didn't. Save yourself some time and heartache and set the boundary. In the personal scenario you identified above, how much time has passed? Is it possible that, by the time you're ready to say something, the offender could potentially have forgotten their actions and the impact they had on you? In the meantime, you agonized over the incident. Take some time to reflect on it now, and how you might approach it next time. Setting boundaries sooner rather than later helps to ensure that you avoid unnecessary angst.

Setting clear boundaries will also depend on your level of comfort with the practice. This is key in determining how to communicate the boundary. We aren't all the same; we may be more comfortable verbalizing our thoughts or we may work better composing our thoughts. Some people are conflict avoidant, so writing their concerns out, while still uncomfortable, might be preferable to having a conversation. Some people are 'bout it, 'bout it so they are ready to have the conversation wherever and whenever. Either one or both are okay—the key is knowing yourself, your comfort level, and what you are trying to accomplish.

Set the Boundary

Once you have determined why you need to set the boundary and the best way to communicate it, then you need to set it. Again, the boundary may be verbal or nonverbal. For example, you receive a meeting request that conflicts with time you have blocked off for yourself. You could respond, orally or in writing, "Unfortunately, I have another appointment at that time. Is there another time we can meet?" The *other* appointment, *your* appointment—that self-care appointment, time-off appointment, mental health day appointment, handling-personal-business appointment—whatever it is, that appointment is important to you, so schedule accordingly. The nonverbal communication here is making an appointment with yourself for the things that are important to you. An example from my own life: My work-day starts at noon. I like having quiet time in the morning, or flexibility to work out, run errands, and so on before I see clients. Of course, I say this as someone who is self-employed and twenty-plus years into their career, so I must acknowledge the freedom and confidence to set boundaries around my time.

For the majority of us who are not self-employed, boundary setting will look different. If you are an employee, that appointment with yourself might mean using vacation or sick time, unpaid leave, or finding coverage for your shift or work responsibilities. Or it may mean not working through your lunch. Or taking breaks throughout the day. Or leaving work at work once the workday is done. The point is to know that you have a right and a responsibility to set boundaries. Others may not like that. But your boundaries are for you.

Finally, if necessary, reset the boundary. Boundary setting is teaching other people how to treat you, and just like any lesson, sometimes it takes folks a few times to finally understand and comply. This is to be expected, albeit frustrating. Know, too, that you may need to change the mode of communication when resetting a boundary. For example, a verbal boundary may need to be reexpressed in an email or vice versa.

As we come to a close, I want to acknowledge again that resetting boundaries can be frustrating and taxing. Clients have shared with me that resetting the boundary was not worth the cost to their well-being. As I told them and will tell you, only you can decide the cost of setting or resetting boundaries. This is why understanding your why for boundary setting is key, because you may determine that the boundary is so important to you that no matter how frustrating it is, it outweighs the frustration of not setting the boundary. Conversely, you may decide that the boundary is not that important and you can live with the boundary violations. You get to decide that, too, because you have choices.

HELPFUL TIPS

- Boundary setting is a skill that requires practice to become proficient. The more proficient you become, the more confident you become.
- Confidence does not necessarily mean comfort. You may continue to experience some discomfort long after you become proficient. For some, it never gets easy. Make sure you prioritize self-care to ensure that the discomfort doesn't become deleterious.
- Remember that the boundaries you set are for you. Do not expect others to respond affirmatively to *your* boundaries.

Chapter 8

FIND YOUR PEOPLE

When I conducted my study of Black women in the workplace in 2014, something in particular became glaringly clear: the need for support and community—and our reluctance as a group to seek that help. During the study, I conducted video-recorded interviews with twelve women to understand their experiences of race and gender stereotypes in the workplace. The study was guided by a primary research question and three sub-research questions. My primary research question was: What are Black working-class women's experiences with race and gender stereotypes in the workplace? My focus on working-class Black women resulted from my discovery that most of the research in this area was based on Black middle- and upper-middle-class women with high-status jobs. Therefore, my research was expanding the literature by including the voices of women who are usually excluded from the canons of knowledge. I mentioned that I also had three sub-questions that guided the interviews, which were: (1) What kinds of race and gender stereotypes do Black working-class women experience in the workplace? (2) How do experiences with race and gender stereotypes in the workplace affect working-class Black women? and (3) How do working-class Black women cope with experiences of race and gender stereotypes in the workplace?

With regard to the last research question about coping, half of the participants reported that giving and receiving support helped them cope with their experiences of race and gender stereotypes at work. For example, some women reported that providing support and encouragement to co-workers dealing with race and gender stereotypes at work helped them cope. One woman stated, in response to a colleague who had approached her for advice, "I told her don't back down...I told her to keep pushing." Another woman said, "I would tell [my co-workers], don't let [our supervisor] say nothing to you to get the best of you."

How many times have you been the anchor or one-person army to a friend, co-worker, or family member who was going through something at work? I know I have had countless "girl, you don't have to take that!" conversations with folks. Giving support represents a type of collective coping that empowers not only the receiver but also the giver. By empowering them, you are empowering yourself. We'll explore this in more detail as we move through this chapter.

During the first year of the COVID-19 pandemic in 2020, I was so relieved to be part of an online community of professional counselors. As a professional community, we were all trying to figure out how to pivot to teletherapy to maintain continuity of care for our clients while simultaneously navigating a pandemic. For me, that online community was a critical source of information, resources, and—importantly—well-being.

Those early days of teletherapy during the pandemic were difficult. The adjustment to the mental and physical impact of the technology was hard. I had to re-create the magic of in-person therapy virtually, although I wasn't totally convinced that I could. My own health concerns made navigating this space more difficult. At the end of the workday, I had terrible headaches, and I was EXHAUSTED. In-person therapy on a typical day with six or seven clients was exhausting on its own. But teletherapy during a pandemic was not typical. And neither was the exhaustion that came with it. Apparently, I wasn't the only one struggling.

Every time I logged onto my online professional community, others shared these same concerns: "Is anyone else exhausted after they see clients?" "Are you all experiencing headaches?" "My back is killing me! Does anybody have a recommendation for a good chair?" The fact that I was not alone in my experiences helped me feel better. You know what I'm talking about. The feels you get when you suddenly realize that you aren't the only one going through a situation. If you were to list the range or assortment of these feelings, I'm sure they would fall into a range of seemingly conflicting feelings (e.g., happiness, sadness, relief, guilt). But can we just agree that the feeling of not being alone in your experience sometimes feels good?

SURVEY SAYS—WE NEED HELP!

For Black women, seeking support from their community is an essential and, it must be acknowledged, evidenced-based way of dealing with race and gender stereotypes at work.

In their article, Angela Neal-Barnett and her research team uncovered the importance of culturally relevant forms of support for Black women.[1] For example, they proposed that sister circles, which are peer support groups for Black women led by Black women centered on a particular topic or issue, can be effective in helping Black women deal with a range of issues (e.g., anxiety, depression, stress) because the presence of other Black women dealing with similar issues reduces the shame and stigma that often hinders help seeking. In their article, which posited the effectiveness of #BlackGirlMagic as a strengths-based framework for treating Black women with depression, researchers Quenette Walton and Olubunmi Oyewuwo-Gassikia found in 2017 that a sense of sisterhood and community promoted healthy coping skills for managing depression.[2] In a 2018 study, J. Camille Hall interviewed 168 Black mothers and daughters to examine how they coped with stress.[3] The study found that support in the form of tangible assistance such as childcare, financial support, and other forms of aid was an essential tool for Black women coping with stress.

In my own research, several women reported that receiving personal and professional support helped them to cope with their experiences at work. Some sought support from family.

One woman stated, "I went home and said something to my son's dad about it and he was like, '[you] need to say something to the job.'" Another woman said, "Me and my dad talked… one thing that he taught me is you have to meet people where they are…let them go be who they are." Other women in the study sought professional support. One woman sought the help of a professional counselor to help her cope with her work experiences. "I ended up reaching out to our EAP [employee assistance program] organization and I went into counseling…" Sometimes the professional support was from co-workers. One woman reported, "I said, God, there's something that I might not be doing right so I went to each individual coach, not only my coach…I [asked] what am I doing to where I am not being promoted so I can change it…and build myself up[?]"

Other researchers have found similar evidence that support in the form of one's faith and spiritual practices help Black women cope with stress. Hall's research examining how Black women cope with stress found that half of the participants in the study relied on their spiritual or religious practices to cope with stress.[4] Eileen Linnabery, Alice Stuhlmacher, and Annette Towler, in their 2014 study that surveyed 188 Black female professionals, found that support from one's church and faith community was a strong predictor of well-being for the participants of the study.[5] In another study in 2014, Aisha Holder, Margo Jackson, and Joseph Ponterotto conducted interviews with Black women in senior-level corporate positions to understand how they coped with racial microaggressions.[6] Their research found that religion and spirituality were a central aspect of support and coping for participants:

> Religion and spirituality provided a sense of empow-
> erment, protection, making sense of things, feel-
> ing grounded, forgiving perpetrators, and serving as a
> reminder that racial microaggressions and other matters
> in the workplace are trivial compared with other issues
> in life.

I also see the salience of faith and spirituality as a significant source of support in my clinical practice. Prayer and meditation are key spiritual practices that my clients report they use
to *armor up* for the beginning of (and throughout) their workday.
I encourage those clients to integrate their spiritual or religious
practices into their overall wellness plan as an effective holistic
approach to navigating race and gender stereotypes at work. If
you identify with faith and spirituality as a core aspect of your
identity and coping, this probably resonates with you on some
level. If so, what practices have you found particularly meaning-
ful and effective at helping you to stay armored up for work (and
life)? What impact do these practices have on you personally
(e.g., mentally, emotionally) and professionally (e.g., interpersonal conflict, boundary violations)? Reflecting on the practices
you use and their effectiveness is critical to feeling empowered
to take care of yourself in difficult moments at work. Equally
important is reflecting on the fact that as Black women it is not

only okay but also necessary to view self-care and support seeking as valuable and viable tools for navigating difficult work
situations—especially when you have been bombarded with
messages that you are, and need to be, strong.

Reflecting on the practices you use and their effectiveness is critical to feeling empowered to take care of
yourself in difficult moments at work.

A PROBLEM STEEPED IN STEREOTYPES

The stereotype of the strong Black woman (SBW), unlike other
stereotypes that emerged from white communities, was believed
to have emerged in the Black community during the 1960s and
1970s civil rights and Black Power movements as resistance to
the intersecting and interlocking forms of oppression that Black
women uniquely experience.[7] Threaded through the narrative of
this resistance was the counternarrative that held Black women
as independent and impervious. However, the prevalence of negative, offensive, and stereotypical depictions of Black women in
the media changed what was once a tool of empowerment into
a tool of oppression that disguises and distorts the multidimensional reality of Black women's lives.

Thanks in part to mediums such as television and film that
depict Black women as aggressive, sassy, and dominant, SBW

became synonymous with another stereotype—the angry Black woman, first popularized in the 1950s by television characters such as Sapphire Stevens on *The Amos 'n Andy Show*, and, later, in the 1970s by Esther Anderson on *Sanford and Son*. Since then, with the exception of television shows such as *Black-ish* and *Queen Sugar*, little has changed with Hollywood's infatuation with casting Black women in negative and stereotypical ways. There is hope for us, though, through the brilliant work of directors and producers Ava DuVernay and Regina King, but we have a long way to go.

The problem with SBW, as with all stereotypes, is that it restricts the full view of Black women's humanity by focusing on *that* they are angry instead of asking the question and waiting for the answer about *why* they might be angry. Let's just agree that there are legitimate reasons for us to be angry, but angry is not all that we are. Strong is not all that we are. We are those things and much more. But one thing is for sure—we are definitely sick and tired of being strong.

A quote from a 2019 study by Jasmine Abrams, Ashley Hill, and Morgan Maxwell to examine the relationship between endorsement of the SBW stereotype and depressive symptoms highlights the negative aspects of this relationship: "Many Black women have mastered the art of portraying strength while concealing trauma—a balancing act often held in high esteem among Black women." For this reason, the majority of Black women may not find seeking support to be obvious or simple.

My own research in this area highlighted how stereotypes are powerful and pervasive in shaping how others perceive and treat us but also how we perceive and treat ourselves. Stereotypes are insidious. Regardless of how aware you are of their existence, stereotypes permeate your psyche in ways that are harmful, and one area this is most evident is in our support-seeking behavior—or lack thereof. This is the danger of stereotypes. They restrict and constrict the full expression of Black women's humanity as both/and. Black women can be independent *and* need help. Black women can be impervious *and* vulnerable. When viewed through the lens of stereotypes, Black women are not only impervious but also inhuman. As such, our cries or calls for help are ignored by others and, worse yet, by us. It is one thing to be silenced by others who don't believe you deserve help. It is yet another thing when you believe them and, therefore, silence yourself. But silent endurance is costly.

Exploring Silent Endurance

Self-silencing, otherwise known as "biting your tongue," is connected to a range of negative health outcomes. As I mentioned earlier, the 2019 study by Abrams, Hill, and Maxwell found a connection between depression and the impact of the SBW stereotype on Black women's tendency to silence themselves.[8] Their study highlighted how Black women with depression who internalized messages of strength based on the SBW stereotype were less likely to seek professional counseling help and therefore silently endured depressive symptoms. A 2010 study conducted by psychologist Cheryl Woods Giscombé found several stress-related behaviors associated with Black women internalizing the SBW stereotype, such as emotional eating, sleep deprivation, poor self-care, migraines, hair loss, and panic attacks.[9] In my doctoral study, self-silencing manifested in the participants as denial, minimization, and rationalization. In discussing how she coped with her experiences of stereotypes at work, one of the participants said, "It's really frustrating and I try not to get myself so frustrated. I always try to think positive 'cause if I think negative then it's just gonna keep bringing me down and I don't want that."

Self-silence represents part of the game that Black women are taught to play at work. But silencing our mouths hurts our minds—and our bodies.

The Body Keeps the Score

By the time some of my Black women clients show up to my office, they are operating on fumes. Stressed out. Overwhelmed. Exhausted. Tired of being sick and tired. Their cup is running over and not in a good way. They are overdue for professional help but did not seek it sooner because they believed they should be able to manage on their own. And further, many believed something had to be wrong with them because they struggled emotionally and mentally while others *seemed* to manage just fine.

And those who did muster up the courage to seek help did not always receive it. "Pray about it," they heard. "Suck it up!" Faced with self-shame and then shame from others, they silently endured until they couldn't—until their bodies wouldn't let them.

Silent endurance leads to loud body talk. That headache that you can't get rid of, the weight you can't lose or gain, the anxiety you feel, the sleep you don't get or get too much of, the stress you feel, that cold that won't go away—that's your body speaking. Our bodies by design are built to survive, and when there is a threat to that survival, they will let you know. We pay with our health and sometimes our lives when we don't listen.

SEEKING SUPPORT

The following is meant to help you seek out and receive effective support when you need it.

First, **determine the goal for support seeking.** I know we don't think about support seeking as a skill, but it is. Whenever you need help, the first thing to consider is the outcome you want. Knowing what you want to achieve is an important aspect in determining the type of support you need.

Ask yourself what specifically you need help with—is it specific to a task or project? Is it more personal or emotional? Consider the following questions: Do I need to vent or do I need a sounding board? Do I need to make a decision? Do I need a solution or an answer? Is the need for support immediate? Does the need require some research?

Create a timeline—this helps make seeking support more tangible, manageable, and attainable. I see failure to set goals as akin to traveling to an unfamiliar location with no directions. You have no idea how to get there or how long it will take. On the other hand, goals help you get where you are trying to go.

Next, **determine the type of support you need**. After you have clarity on your goals for seeking support, it's now important to determine the type of support you need, whether personal, professional, or both; and informal or formal.

- Personal support includes intimate partners, family, friends, online communities—people whom you have relationships with outside the context of work or school; people whom you don't pay in exchange for therapeutic services. Be thoughtful about whom you approach—talking to someone who is a problem solver will not help you if you just need to vent. Confiding in someone who is a known gossip might lead to your business getting out where you don't want it. Avoid taking your problems on a listening tour. Seeking support and guidance from too many people leads to confusion, frustration, and indecision. Be clear on what you want to accomplish, and choose the best person to help you accomplish it—in this case, those who have demonstrated trustworthiness and a respect for privacy.

- Professional support may be formal or informal support. *Informal* professional support can include co-workers, mentors or coaches, and online professional communities (e.g., Facebook groups). *Formal* support may include co-workers, human resources, or professional affiliations (e.g., unions, associations). Formal third-party support such as the Equal Employment Opportunity Commission (EEOC), a federal agency that enforces civil rights laws against workplace discrimination, harassment, and retaliation claims—and other support such as employment or workplace discrimination attorneys—can also be instrumental in helping you address instances where your civil or labor rights have been violated.

After determining the goal and identifying what kind of support you need, you'll **initiate support seeking**. Sometimes the hardest step is reaching out. How many times have you talked yourself out of getting help? Those unhealthy, unhelpful, and untrue thoughts will have you saying things like, "Nobody can help me with this." Or "I don't want to be a burden because they have their own problems." Thoughts like that can immobilize you and perpetuate silent endurance. But silent endurance stops today! Ask, seek, and knock until you get the help you need.

A simple formula to initiate seeking support is:

problem + *outcome* + *ask*.

For example, you decided to reach out to your friend about a recent situation at work involving a disagreement with your supervisor, and you wanted to have a follow-up conversation with the supervisor to address some things that were said but are unsure of how to broach the topic. Using the formula above, that conversation might look something like this: "Girl, me and my supervisor had a meeting about my performance, and she said some things that made me feel disrespected (problem). I want to let her know how she made me feel, but I am not sure how to say how I felt without making things worse (outcome). How can I express to her how the conversation made me feel in a way that is productive and not destructive (ask)?"

Many of my clients struggle deeply when it comes to communicating their needs. Often, this is because they are afraid of a negative response—"What if they say no?" Or they struggle with how to put their problem into words. To this first fear, it's important to know that you cannot control how people respond. You also cannot let the fear of how others respond control you. There are a number of factors that contribute to someone's response to you, and most of them have nothing to do with you. Their response is out of your control. What is in your control is how you communicate what you need. Sometimes we don't get what we need because we haven't clearly communicated our needs. One of the biggest misconceptions about communication is assuming that communication has occurred! Work on communicating clearly. Use the above formula as a guide, or write out what you want to say ahead of time.

HAVE GRACE FOR YOUR PACE

I want you to know that it is okay to not be okay. You are not going to be okay every day or all the time, and that is okay. You're human. It is also okay to get support when you're not okay. Sometimes you will be able to manage distress or difficulties on your own. If what you are doing is working, then keep doing it. However, if what you are doing does not work or you need someone to support you as you go through and work through, that is okay too. You are not a superwoman. You do not have some magical and mythical ability to overcome adversity. You and I both know that what looks easy to others was hard-earned behind the scenes.

I also want you to know that you are not alone. I include research and clinical insights in this book because I want to affirm that the issues you may be having at work (and in life) are real and valid, but also collective. I want you to know that you have a village of sistas—among them Black women researchers and clinicians who see and understand your pain because it is also their pain. Your village recognizes the importance of information and inspiration to ignite you to live a life where you move beyond surviving to flourishing. You do not have to endure alone. We got you!

Looking ahead, we will discuss how to navigate when shit gets real at work. We will provide you with effective and proven tools to advocate for yourself should you have conflict with a co-worker or boss as well as tools to navigate if your civil or employee rights have been violated.

HELPFUL TIPS

- Not everybody in your circle is in your corner. Surround yourself with the right people.
- Silent endurance is not a badge of honor. It will cost you more than it helps you.
- Keep asking, keep seeking, and keep knocking, because you are worth the effort.

Chapter 9

BATTLE WISELY

I come from generations of women who were fighters. Literally and figuratively, the women in my family fought to protect themselves, their families, and as I shared in chapter 1, their respect. My mother, grandmother, and great-grandmother did not take shit from anyone. There was hell to pay for anyone who crossed them. Fighting is strength, and in a world where Black women like my mother and grandmothers are often mistreated and disrespected, fighting is not optional. In the Bible, Ecclesiastes 3:8 tells us that there is a time for peace and there is a time for war. Unfortunately for Black women, we don't always choose the war. Sometimes, the war chooses us.

For the record, I do not like to fight. I never have. When I was eight or nine years old, a boy in the neighborhood approached me wanting to fight. I have no idea why. It was probably some silly reason like he liked me but I didn't like him. Whatever this kid's reason, he wanted to fight me, and I was terrified. He was bigger than me and he was a boy, so to me that meant I was about to get beat up. I decided I needed a plan.

In my neighborhood, you got picked on and beat up if you were scared, so I couldn't back down and risk more threats from other kids. I stormed into my house "looking" for a stick. My mama, who was home at the time, must have noticed me looking like I was looking for something. She asked, "Tammy, what you are looking for?"

"A stick."

"A stick for what?"

"This boy outside wanna fight me, so I need a stick!"

Mama said, "Well, ain't no stick in here. If you don't get your ass out there and fight that boy, I'ma whup your ass!"

Not exactly what I had in mind.

She was the "stick" I was looking for. My plan was, I needed backup. Instead, I was forced to go outside and fight the boy. To make matters worse, she marched right behind me to make sure that I did. I was so scared! I didn't want to fight, but I for sure didn't want to get my ass whupped. My mama yelled, "Hit him!" I started swinging my arms like a windmill, which landed a punch or two. I was doing it—I was fighting!

The boy punched me squarely in my eye. "Ouuuuch!" I yelled. Crying, I turned around and ran inside. That was it. Fight was over. I was mad at Mama for making me fight and even more so because I got punched in the eye. But I think she was preparing me for a future reality that I did not yet know but she knew all too well.

Though the fistfights continued throughout my childhood and adolescence, a different fight emerged in adulthood: work. And, though the fight was different, some things remained the same. As a Black woman, I still had to fight when I didn't want to, or ran the risk of figuratively getting my ass whupped. The fight with the neighborhood boy taught me a valuable lesson— knowing how to fight takes skills. And when the fight is experiences of discrimination at work, many of us haven't learned the skills. If you grew up in the inner city like me, you probably were "taught" to fight the same way I was. But you and I both know that you cannot be snatching people up at work, although you might really want to or they might really deserve it.

SELF-ADVOCACY: THE MIDPOINT

When I talk about fighting at work, what I am really talking about is coping. And coping exists on a continuum. On one end is silence and on the other end is snap (i.e., snatch), and neither is effective. The midpoint is self-advocacy. Self-advocacy refers to speaking up and speaking out against interpersonal and institutional experiences of race and gender stereotypes at work.

Self-advocacy is an effective and evidenced-based coping skill for navigating race and gender stereotypes at work. In 2012, psychologist Jioni Lewis and her research team conducted a study to examine the coping strategies of seventeen Black women college students who experienced gendered racial micro-aggressions.[1] Lewis and her team found that self-advocacy was a powerful coping strategy used by study participants to help them regain power in situations where experiences rooted in race and gender stereotypes (e.g., gendered racial microaggressions) made them feel powerless.

The women in my study also expressed the use of self-advocacy as a powerful tool to cope with race and gender stereotypes at work.[2] For some, self-advocacy occurred at the interpersonal level (e.g., co-workers and supervisors). One woman stated:

It was this one [white man], I can't remember what he said to me, but he said something to me...I looked at him like he was crazy—he looked at me—[and] I said don't talk to me like that no more....I told [him he] was racist.

Other women in the study described advocating for themselves at the institutional level (e.g., through human resources). Another participant, who was demoted after she changed her hair from chemically processed hairstyles to natural hairstyles, shared:

I [came] in at 8:00 [to speak] to somebody at human resources and tell them what I feel and this time I bring up the hair...human resources [says], "We're gonna investigate this. We take this serious. This is a form of harassment. It's not sexual harassment but if this is what's going on it's a violation of our policy. No, we don't have anything in here about hair but we do have something in here about people treating you differently."

Thus, self-advocacy, unlike self-silence, empowers us to use our voices to challenge as well as cope with harmful experiences at work. The key with self-advocacy, like most skills, is knowing what you want to accomplish and how best to accomplish it.

THE CROWN ACT

Unfortunately for Black women, the right to wear hairstyles that don't conform to white standards of beauty or professionalism is also a battle we must fight at work. Wearing our hair in natural or protective styles has led to experiences of hair discrimination at work that affect us personally and professionally. In 2019, the Dove CROWN Research Study surveyed two thousand women in the US and found that 80 percent of Black women reported that they have had to change their hair from its natural state to fit in at work.[3] The study also found that Black women are one and a half times more likely to be sent home because of their hair.

Several of the participants in my study also expressed the role that "Black hairstyles" contributed to their experiences of discrimination in the workplace.[4] One participant shared:

Your hair play a part. If you wear that loud weave...nobody gone hire you...somebody wear that loud weave that's hot pink...oh she got to be ghetto. That [don't] mean that...you can't [say that] by looking at these people hair...other races—Mexican, white, Chinese...they can have spiked hair and be in the corporate business...we can't do that. Soon as you get a step up by going towards that way they tell you tone your hair down...show it to me in y'all policy where it say I got to wear my hair a certain way.

While these findings may be disheartening, I am willing to bet they are not surprising.

What I said at the beginning of the book bears repeating: Our hair can be a situation—especially at work. Think about your own experiences. Have you experienced situations at work where a particular hairstyle led to an uncomfortable conversation ("Your hair looks *different!*"), experience (the meeting to discuss the *appropriateness* of your appearance), or just a feeling (worried that your hairstyle might present a challenge)? I know I have.

One memory stands out about a situation involving my hair in the workplace. It was 2007, and I had been promoted to a leadership position that I'd been working really hard to get. At that time, my hair was natural and dyed cherry red, which I thought was fire (no pun intended), but I wasn't sure as the only Black woman in my department how my colleagues who were all white would feel. Were they going to think my hair was *ghetto* or—worse—that I was *ghetto*?

I requested a meeting to speak with my new supervisor, a white woman, to ask her if my hair was going to be "a problem." She seemed confused by the question—almost like the question in her head was "Is *this* why we are meeting—to discuss your *hair*?" But I got it. As a white woman, she didn't have to think about her hair as a stumbling block up the career ladder. But as a Black woman, I did. Although I had worked hard to earn the promotion, there was still a fear that my natural fiery red hair that I loved could somehow hinder me professionally in the long run. No Black woman should have to experience this type of fear—ever! But we do, and that fear is real and valid because we know our hair can be a problem, especially in predominantly white workplaces.

As Black women, our hair is not only our crown and glory but a right. In 2019, four Black women leaders, Esi Eggleston Bracey, Kelli Richardson Lawson, Orlena Nwokah Blanchard, and Adjoa B. Asamoah, led the CROWN Act movement to end race-based hair discrimination.[5] The CROWN (Creating a Respectable and Open World for Natural Hair) Act, first signed into law on July 3, 2019, in California, prohibits race-based hair discrimination against natural or protective hairstyles that lead to denial of employment or educational opportunities. To date, fourteen states have passed the CROWN Act. (Unfortunately, it was not passed in my home state of Louisiana, but it was passed in my hometown of New Orleans!) While this is a step in the right direction, the journey is long and the struggle for hair equality continues.

PREPARING FOR BATTLE

I want to give you an in-depth look at my experience with workplace discrimination as a map that can help you navigate similar situations should you encounter them in your workplace. We will also review strategies to effectively navigate conflicts you may have with the folks you work with.

When I dealt with workplace discrimination, I had to determine what I was actually fighting for and, more importantly, whether what I was fighting for was worth it. I had to ask myself *why* I was fighting: "Am I fighting for my job? Am I fighting because my ego is bruised? Am I fighting for my rights? What's the fight?" I determined that my name, my rights, and my reputation were worth the fight.

I felt that I could no longer work at my job and feel safe.

I was aware of how the company's HR handled previous complaints in favor of the company, so my goal was to ensure that my complaints would not be ignored or dismissed. That meant instead of HR, I took my complaint straight to the EEOC. But before I did, I did my homework.

I researched EEOC policies and procedures to understand whether my experience fit their definition of discrimination and to further understand the EEOC's power to advocate and take legal action on my behalf, if necessary. I was taking a big step by bringing my claims to the federal agency that administers and enforces civil rights laws on workplace discrimination. I had to be prepared for such a big fight and what it could mean.

The EEOC was a neutral yet powerful advocate, and that was what I needed. When Sofia, the supervisor at the Charlotte EEOC office, approved to file a charge of race discrimination on my behalf, I knew I had the power. If a mutual agreement could not be found between me and the company, the EEOC had the power to file a lawsuit on my behalf. But I knew I didn't want to take it that far. By the time I got the EEOC involved, I was already mentally and physically exhausted from the whole ordeal, so a lawsuit was out of the question. An EEOC charge of race discrimination was sufficient. An email from the HR director at the time confirmed that it was the first time that an employee's allegations of discrimination actually led to an EEOC charge of race discrimination. Apparently previous allegations could not be substantiated. But this was a fight I was willing to have, and I was prepared to have it.

Self-Advocacy in Contradiction

Self-advocacy at work as a Black woman is tricky because we are often trying to achieve two contradictory goals. That is, fighting for our rights without losing our minds. My experience of workplace discrimination started because I advocated for myself by challenging a verbal write-up about nonsense that could only be explained as stereotyping and bias. Had I just shut my mouth and signed the damn write-up, there would have been no retaliation. There would have been no EEOC involvement and relatedly no mental and physical anguish. Of course, I could not have predicted how things unfolded. If I knew at the outset what I learned in hindsight, I believe I would do the same thing all over again. I knew what I was fighting for and why. I didn't choose all that came with the fight, but I made the best possible choices to take care of myself during that experience with the knowledge I did have. The point that I am making here is that self-advocacy has its benefits. But it also has its consequences.

Advocating for yourself can cause you to be *conflicted*. The mental anguish of my experience was exacerbated by feelings of doubt and uncertainty about whether I was doing the right thing and whether my perception of the events was accurate and valid. For me to go through that process and come out with my mind intact, it was important and necessary for me to listen to my body's signs that I was unwell and respond by using many of the tools that I share with you in this book.

Advocating for yourself can also lead to conflict in your work relationships, conflict with workplace policies and practices, or retaliation. The nature of the conflict will likely determine how you to choose to address it. If you have conflict with a co-worker or supervisor, you might choose to have a conversation with that person. Ongoing interpersonal conflict or a rights violation might warrant a formal complaint to a third party like HR (more on that later) or the EEOC, respectively. But regardless of the nature of the conflict, can we just agree that conflict is stressful? Unless you just like conflict—and those folks do exist—it is safe to say that most people try to avoid it, which is why some folks choose to just let things go. But I've found that going along to get along is stressful too. Whether you advocate for yourself or not, there is a cost and you get to decide which cost you can and will bear.

The HR Conundrum

Despite a company's claim to protect employees' rights and fairness in the process, the truth is sometimes that's a lie. Especially if you are a Black woman. The last thing a company wants to hear is you complain about mistreatment on the basis of—stereotypes?! They will do everything in their power to make you doubt the validity of your experience, and before long, you start to do the same. And if you don't doubt your experience, you might doubt whether self-advocacy is the right step. Remember this: Your decision to self-advocate should not hinge on the question of whether you are worth the fight. You are. All day. Every day. Rather, what's important in the decision to self-advocate is what you are trying to accomplish and the most effective—that is, healthy and helpful—way to do that.

SELF-ADVOCACY IN PRACTICE

The following sections will offer strategies and helpful tips to promote effective self-advocacy at work. Note that you will learn strategies that are helpful to address interpersonal and institutional issues at work and some that are specific to interpersonal relationships.

Interpersonal and Institutional Self-Advocacy

First, **know your goals**. Perhaps this goes without saying, because it's become a theme—but it bears repeating. Know what your goals for self-advocacy are. Remember, the goal should not be to determine your worth. If you are looking for the same employer whose actions invalidated you in the first place to affirm you, you've already lost the fight. You are worth the fight. Period. Beyond that, what do you want the outcome of your self-advocacy to be? Self-advocacy has two levels: interpersonal and institutional.

Confronting a co-worker or supervisor about a racist comment or offensive joke is an example of self-advocacy at the

interpersonal level. On the other hand, voicing concerns to an institutional entity about an interpersonal issue (e.g., conflict with a supervisor) or institutional issue (e.g., unfair workplace policies or practices) is an example of advocacy at the **institutional level**. Thus, self-advocacy at this level might involve institutional entities (e.g., HR) or formal processes (e.g., filing a grievance or complaint). At the institutional level, understanding workplace policies can be instrumental in helping you prepare to advocate. For example, knowing the *written* policy regarding filing grievances can help answer certain questions that might otherwise hinder you from taking action. Have you read your workplace's employee handbook? Do your research! Knowing your goals (and what you are getting into) helps you to be more effective and efficient in your self-advocacy.

It will be necessary to **provide tangible evidence**. So many discrimination claims go uninvestigated due to a lack of evidence. When it was time for me to meet with my supervisor, the company attorney, and the chief human resource officer at the EEOC meeting, you would have thought I was Perry Mason for real. I came ready for battle. I had a binder full of evidence with printed emails, documented conversations with dates and who was involved, EEOC laws and policies regarding workplace discrimination, research on the impact of stereotypes, prior reviews that demonstrated my high performance, and positive feedback on surveys from teams that I worked with. I even had an outline of the evidence so that I could easily refer to it during the meeting! When I looked across the table, the attorney had a blank yellow legal pad, and the other two had worried looks on their faces. By the end of the meeting, they all learned that I was smarter than I looked, and I covered my ass well.

Maybe being a counselor had something to do with my level of preparation, but facts and details are always important when advocating for yourself. Dates, times, and event details are critical pieces of information because an employer can easily dispute your feelings. It is much harder to dispute the facts (well, at least this was true before 2016). And when it comes to Black women advocating for themselves, tangible and concrete information is critical, because it is expected that our only tool for battle is anger. If anger is your only tool, it is easy to dismiss. It's harder to dismiss the facts. And when it comes to self-advocacy, feelings alone are not enough. Let's look at a case example:

Nicole is a twenty-five-year-old Black woman who has worked for six months as a part-time cashier in a department store. Nicole is frustrated with Diane, her supervisor, because Nicole has asked Diane to schedule her for more hours, but Diane denies the request because "extra hours aren't available." Meanwhile, Nicole has noticed that the new white female part-time cashier, Amber, who has been employed at the store for only a month, consistently gets more hours on the schedule. Nicole is aware of similar treatment from Diane toward two other Black women in the department and decides she wants to confront Diane about her "racist behavior." Nicole likes working at the department store but knows that she will have to find another job if she can't get the hours she needs.

Put yourself in Nicole's shoes—what approach would you take to address Diane? Would your approach help or hinder your goal of getting more hours and ultimately keeping your job? Did you say your approach would be a hindrance? It's okay if you did. You're not alone.

Here is an example of an effective way Nicole could approach Diane. "Diane, I wanted to meet with you because I submitted several requests during our individual meetings (facts/details) for more hours back in July and August (facts). You denied my request because 'extra hours weren't available' (facts/quote) but I noticed on the schedule that Amber is also part-time (facts) but has been getting more hours than me (observation) even though she just started a month ago (facts). Are there other reasons why my requests are being denied? I like working here but I really need more hours." What do you think the outcome would be?

What do you think the outcome would be if Nicole approached Diane and said, "Diane, I've been asking you for more hours but instead you're giving all the hours to Amber! You're only doing that because you're racist!"

The truth is, Diane might be racist, but if Nicole has determined that getting more hours and keeping her job are her goals, her communication style may not achieve those goals. As I will discuss in the next section, effective communication is key to self-advocacy.

One important thing to keep in mind about self-advocacy: Don't focus on the outcome. Your power isn't in the outcome.

You could provide all the evidence in the world, and it still might not lead to the outcome you want. The power is in using your voice. Attaching to outcomes can leave you feeling more dejected and devalued, especially if the outcomes aren't favorable. Regardless of the perceived outcome, speak up and speak out anyway. Therein lies your power.

Interpersonal Self-Advocacy

Have you ever heard the saying "hurt people hurt people"? It's true. This is why it's important to **speak without offending and listen without defending**. When we are hurting emotionally or mentally, sometimes we unconsciously and consciously hurt others. When the hurt is conscious, the need to hurt others can help us feel powerful in an otherwise powerless situation. Have you ever experienced a time when someone said or did something to you that hurt your feelings, your ego, or your pride, and for a split second you thought about ways you could get back at that person or make them feel what you felt? The feeling of powerlessness in that situation, albeit not conscious, was there operating underneath the surface. When these situations happen at work, that sense of powerlessness doesn't dissipate, especially if it compounds feelings of powerlessness outside of work. These moments can lead to ineffective communication, where in our attempt to advocate for ourselves, we speak to offend, and listen to defend. Knowing your triggers and regulating your emotions, using "I" statements, and seeking clarity and understanding are steps you can take to effectively communicate your workplace concerns.

- Know Your Triggers and Regulate Your Emotions: This is a critical aspect of effective self-advocacy. Triggers can cause us to lose control and react in ways that are not healthy or helpful. During times of conflict at work, knowing your triggers can help you be proactive in managing your emotions, maintaining control, and ultimately avoiding saying or doing something you will regret later. If someone yelling at you is a trigger, setting a boundary to let the person know that you will exit the conversation if the yelling continues or actually exiting the conversation might be the thing to do to take care of your feelings. Knowing what your triggers are beforehand facilitates your ability to take care of yourself in the moment or moments after. Take a moment to identify some of your triggers.

- Use "I" Statements: The use of "I" statements is another effective communication tool for self-advocacy. When you use "I" statements versus "you" statements, you are asserting your position without blaming the other person. When a person feels blame, they get defensive, and that defensiveness leads to unproductiveness. "I" statements, like tangible evidence, are hard to dispute. If you told your co-worker or supervisor, "You were disrespectful," that person could challenge the idea that their behavior was disrespectful. But the statement "I felt disrespected" could not be challenged, because the person could not tell you how you felt. Thus, using "I" statements is an effective communication tool to advocate for your needs and concerns at work.

- Seek Clarity and Understanding: It bears repeating that one of the biggest problems with communication is assuming that communication happened in the first place. Conflict often arises because of miscommunication where one or both parties are responding to the perceived message versus the actual message. I see this issue often when I work with couples to build effective communication skills. One partner will say something, and then the person listening will repeat back, often incorrectly, what they heard the other one say, which leads to conflict in the session. Part of my work with these couples is helping them see the connection between what they heard versus what was said—and then teaching them how to listen to understand, convey that understanding to their partner, and, when necessary, clarify the misunderstanding. This approach is very helpful at work too. Seeking clarity and understanding is an effective tool for communicating your needs and concerns because it creates consistency between the perceived message and the actual message. Some examples of how to seek clarity and understanding are: "When you said ___, what I heard was___. Is that what you meant?" Or "I heard you say____. Did I hear that right?" Or "Something is not connecting for me. What am I missing or not understanding?"

Being in control of your words and actions is powerful. You have the power not to let others control what you think, feel, and do. You have the power to speak up and speak out. Own your power and let it be known.

KNOWING YOUR WORTH

Using your voice is power. But knowing *how to* use your voice to your advantage, especially at work, is more powerful. For centuries, race and gender stereotypes of Black women have led to our voices being silenced, ignored, shut up, and shut out in the workplace. We have been told that our voices didn't matter because our humanity didn't matter. Unfortunately, when you hear this kind of messaging long enough, you not only start to believe that it is true but, worse yet, you also become complicit in your own oppression and suppression. When you advocate for yourself, you amplify that you are not willing to play a game where your happiness, health, and humanity do not matter. Nope. It's a new game in town. A game where we not only know our worth but show our worth.

In the final chapter of this book, we will discuss how to navigate decisions about whether to stay at or leave a work environment that may not be the best or healthiest for you. We will explore how to make work work for you when leaving is not an option, as well as how to know when it's time to go.

HELPFUL TIPS

- There's a time to be silent and a time to speak up and speak out. Knowing how and when to do each is important.
- Your voice is your power. Don't let anyone silence it, including you!
- You are always worth the fight, but the fight may not always be worth it to you. Knowing the difference is half the battle!

Chapter 10

KNOW WHEN TO HOLD AND WHEN TO WALK AWAY

The decision to stay in or leave a job creates unique challenges. Sometimes the challenges are personal. As Black women, we make decisions about work that may have consequences that extend beyond us. Many of us have financial or family obligations that can cause us to feel stuck in a toxic work situation. I see this with so many clients who worry about being viewed as selfish or irresponsible if they leave a job for reasons that others may not deem sufficient. If you've been in this situation, you probably know this feeling all too well. Unfortunately, when you are expected to be a strong Black woman, leaving a job to maintain your mental and physical health is not a good enough reason for some.

In this chapter, we will discuss strategies for you to be more confident in your decision-making to stay in or leave a job.

Deciding to stay or leave can be overwhelming and downright immobilizing, which often leads folks to end up stuck in a job longer than they want or need to be. Maybe you are in a situation where you are feeling the pull to leave. Maybe the work environment is toxic, and you've had enough. Or, maybe, you're in a dead-end job situation where opportunities to advance are practically nonexistent. Maybe you're ready to move into an entirely different job or career path altogether that reflects where you are trying to go, not where you've been. Perhaps you are faced with a work situation where you want to stay because you love the work but don't love the people you work with. Or maybe you don't love the work but leaving is not an option. Wherever you are on the continuum to stay or leave, this chapter will provide you with valuable and practical strategies that will help you own your decisions with confidence.

Before we explore the strategies later in the chapter, I want to share a story with you about my decision in 2019 to leave an academic position and, quite frankly, my last time working for someone else. My decision to walk away was me trusting God and betting on (and taking care of) me. Game over. Of course, I recognize that you might not be in a position to walk away from your job. But my hope for you is that through my story, you will understand that at the end of the day, the decision to stay in or leave a job is ultimately rooted in the thread that runs through this book: You've got to know your worth and prioritize your wellness for you to thrive and be well at work—and beyond.

I'M GONNA DO ME

In 2015, I accepted a full-time visiting assistant professor position in the graduate counseling department at the University of New Orleans. After twelve years away, I was excited to return to my hometown and serve my community with my talents, time, and treasure. I was also proud to return home as a married woman, a mother of two, and a doctor. The granddaughter of "the help," the daughter of a teenage mother and single, divorced woman was now a professor! Their sacrifices paid off.

Teaching came particularly easy to me because I was teaching about a profession that I had worked in for fifteen years and knew a whole lot about. I brought a range of clinical, professional, specialized training, as well as leadership experiences and passion to the classroom. I also brought a concern about the future outlook of the counseling profession. Encounters with fragile and incompetent clinicians along my professional journey were the reason I pursued doctoral education in the first place. I brought these concerns to my classroom, bearing in mind that master's-level counseling programs are meant to prepare future professional counselors to engage in the business of caring for others. At the outset, I was transparent with administrators, colleagues, and students that I was there to be a gatekeeper of the profession and train future ethical, culturally responsive, competent, and confident professional counselors. My role would involve educating, evaluating, and, if necessary, eliminating those who were not up to the task. I worked to make this evident in my syllabi, course assignments, classroom expectations, and feedback and evaluations. Doing so was important to me because a poorly trained or ill-suited counselor can be disastrous for future clients. I made it clear that that was not going to happen on my watch!

That first year, I taught a course on diagnosis; for the midterm, students were required to determine a client's issue based on a case study. This is a required, core competency area, and students often struggle with it, as diagnosis requires the ability to assess for a range of factors and symptoms and accurately render a diagnosis. However, diagnosis is not an exact science, and much depends on the ability to *do it right*. For high-achieving graduate counseling students, doing it right mostly means earning As. Unfortunately for most of the students that spring semester, they were lucky if they earned Cs on the midterm evaluation. Despite my attempts to accept some responsibility and assure them that they would have more opportunities to practice and develop diagnosis skills over the semester, my mostly white, female students were not having it. The next thing I knew, I was called in to meet with the dean and department chair, a white man and woman, respectively.

The meeting did not go well. Not only was I essentially asked to change grades in the meeting, but I was also accused of being "militant" and "scaring the students." The dean repeatedly ignored, minimized, and challenged my competence as junior faculty. I asserted that while I might have been new to teaching, I was new neither to the counseling profession nor to providing evaluation and feedback. The dean was not having it! He was intent on putting me in my place, which, as a visiting assistant professor and Black woman, was at the bottom. At some point I realized my attempts were not working, so I asked him, "What do you recommend that I do to resolve this?" Seems like a fair question, right? I thought so too. I assumed that since he clearly thought that the midterm grades were a reflection of my incompetence and inexperience, then as dean he could offer up some wisdom. His reply: "That's what you need to figure out." I was done. I turned to the chair, who had been silent during the entire meeting, and asked, "Are we done here? Because I am." She tried to reignite the conversation, but I meant what I said. I was done. Anything out of my mouth would have been a windmill of words, and some of those words were sure to land.

The meeting with the department chair and dean marked the first time in academia of students going above my head to complain to the administration or weaponizing evaluations. It was also the first sign that the administration did not have my back. If things were going to get better, I'd have to figure out how to make them better.

After the second year of teaching, a shift occurred. This was the result of increasing efforts to be more transparent about my teaching philosophy and methods, which I think helped the students and administration to understand that I wasn't an angry Black woman with a personal agenda to scare students and make them miserable. I was firm but fair. Eventually, word spread that my courses were rigorous and that my unapologetic and true agenda was to train future professional counselors who were ethical, culturally responsive, confident, and competent. Things were starting to settle down, and I was beginning to think that I might be able to settle down too.

My position was a renewable yearly contract that would eventually end, so, when a tenure-track vacancy opened up the following year, I looked forward to the chance for a few years of job stability. Given the challenges of the previous year, I wasn't wholly confident in my chances, but I still applied, and though I was disappointed when I was denied the position, I was not surprised.

Although an opportunity for my existing position to be converted to tenure-track opened up the following year, I was denied. This time, however, my disappointment was replaced by anger—I knew if I'd had the support and backing of the department chair and dean, the outcome would have been much different. In that moment, I knew there was no way I could survive and thrive in an environment where there was no support.

I also had battle scars from my previous fight as a senior clinical leader. The emotional and physical wounds from that experience were still palpable, and I was not about to jeopardize my well-being or peace trying to prove to the academy that I belonged there. I was satisfied that I had done what I came there to do. In my final meeting with the department chair, we discussed my departure from the program. She was baffled when I disclosed in the meeting that I would work through the summer but would not be reapplying for an upcoming tenure-track position.

"Well, what are you gonna do?"

"I'm gonna do *me*."

Looking confused, she asked, "You're gonna do what?"

"Me. I have my own business and I have many exciting things that I am working on in my business. Thank you for the opportunity, but my time is up here. I'm proud of the work that I've done, so I'm good."

And with that, the meeting was over. I left that meeting feeling like a million bucks because I did something that day that sometimes as Black women we don't get to do—leave on our own terms.

THE DECISION AIN'T EASY

Deciding to leave a job has its own unique challenges. Beyond the financial impact, questions about when to leave or where to go also create challenges. There never seems to be a good time to leave a job. There is always some financial or family obligation that makes staying sound better. Then there's the fear. Fear of the unknown makes it hard for a lot of us to leave, because staying and dealing with the hell you know can feel safer than going to the hell you don't know. When we don't have sufficient knowledge about something, we tend to fill in the gaps with negative information. This is true whether we have evidence for those beliefs or not. Beyond that, I've witnessed and personally experienced the guilt and shame that we sometimes feel when have to make work decisions for our own well-being that affect our families and loved ones. In this section, we'll explore a few of the main challenges we face when deciding to leave the workplace—be it because the work environment is toxic, or we've gone as far as we can and it's time to move on.

Your Economic Lifeline

Much of my mental anguish before I resigned from the job in Charlotte was due to worrying about how we would survive financially if I left my job. Because I was married, and once I realized I didn't have to figure everything out on my own, I could discuss it with my husband—this became a problem for us to solve together. However, if you are on your own or have limited personal resources, your decision might require you to seek support from your support systems. Who in your support network could provide you with short-term or long-term financial assistance if necessary? Maybe a change in job might lead to changes in your housing situation (e.g., stability, affordability). If that is the case, consider what options you would have for housing (e.g., living with someone temporarily, having a roommate to offset costs, downsizing). One of the things that became apparent to me and my husband after I resigned was that we could no longer afford the plush and spacious apartment we lived in. We had to make the tough decision to downsize to an apartment that was more affordable and smaller. It was a temporary and short-term sacrifice, so we made it work. Remember, your perspective matters. How you view your situation will determine how you feel about it. Viewing a temporary sacrifice for a long-term gain down the line can be a valuable perspective to get you through a tough decision like leaving your job.

Minding Your Body and Brain

If you decide to stay in a toxic work environment, or else you are unable to just leave your job, all of your self-care and self-empowerment skills may not be enough to stay and thrive in a work environment where you are overworked, overlooked, underpaid, and undervalued. Further, work environments in which there is constant threat of interpersonal conflict or institutional challenges put you in a constant state of flight or fight. Constant fighting is exhausting and stressful. The saying "What don't kill you makes you stronger" is a lie. Stress kills, and if it doesn't kill you, it makes you sicker. Yet the reality is we can't always leave no matter how much we want or need to.

When you are faced with these circumstances, many of the strategies already discussed are valuable to help you survive until you can thrive. While self-care alone may not be enough to get you through, it is essential. As we discussed in chapter 4, there are basic things your body needs to survive regardless of what is happening in your environment. When self-care is not prioritized, not only does it make functioning optimally in your current job harder, but it also makes having clarity of mind and motivation to find a new job hard. We also discussed the value of professional counseling in chapter 5 as a valuable tool for dealing with work situations. A professional counselor can help you gain valuable insights about how to cope within your current environment and help you work through an eventual exit plan. Relatedly, engaging your support systems can also help you navigate a difficult decision to remain in a toxic work environment. Having a supportive network at work or at home may not change your situation, but there is therapeutic value in having people you trust that you can confer with and confide in about work. Finally, having a timeline ("I'm going to give myself six months to find a new job") or a particular goal you want to achieve while remaining in your current job ("I will stay and earn my certification because it will make me more marketable when I do look for a job") can be an effective approach to your decision to stay. Timelines and goals give you something to work toward and help to minimize the feeling of being stuck.

Fear of the Unknown

Fear is a real and valid emotion, and when the fear is of the unknown, it can be immobilizing. If you ever experienced this type of fear, then you know it can stop you in your tracks and block any forward movement. When that fear is leaving a job you know to search for a new job (that you don't have yet), this is just as true. You might have questions like "What if I don't find a job?" "What if I find a job but they want to pay me less and I don't have good benefits?" If you have children or other caregiving responsibilities, you might wonder, "Will I find a job that will work with my schedule at home?" Again, these concerns are real and valid; however, just because you don't have the answer to those questions does not mean that the answers are necessarily negative. It is just as possible that you will find a job that pays more and has good benefits and will be flexible enough to allow you to take care of your family or obligations.

When I've worked with clients who are grappling with fear about leaving their job, they all were struck by my asking simple questions like "What evidence do you have that leaving will be worse?" or "Is it possible that you could leave and find something better for you?" The beauty of those simple questions is that they yield profound answers: "None" and "Yes," respectively. But fear stops us from asking questions that might free us to go in another direction that might allow us to be well and excel.

Fear is a real and valid emotion, and when the fear is of the unknown, it can be immobilizing.

Taking a step back to assess the accuracy of your thoughts can be helpful in dealing with the fear of the unknown. One way to do this is by asking yourself, "Do I have evidence for my fear?" If you do have evidence that the fear is real, ask yourself,

"What is in my control to address the thing that I am fearful about? If you do not have evidence for your fear, then ask yourself, "What is one step that I can take today to push past the fear?" Think of the one step as one thing you can do that is low risk, at low or no cost to you, that you can do (e.g., conducting an online job search, talking to a trusted support, working on your résumé). And, of course, discussing your fears with a professional counselor can also help you to challenge inaccurate, unhealthy, and unhelpful thoughts that might be contributing to the fear.

Workplace Relationships

In addition to the strain on our mental and physical health, decisions to stay in a work environment where we've experienced race and gender stereotypes may also lead to strained interpersonal relationships. This is particularly true when you advocate for yourself. If you've ever spoken up for yourself, you know how people change. As Black women we are often expected to shut up and be grateful that we have a job. When we start complaining about being treated unfairly, we may be subject to harassment or retaliation, or we have to deal with the distance—co-workers distancing themselves from us or the felt need to distance ourselves from them. Distance in any relationship kills the relationship. It is hard to maintain a healthy workplace relationship where the communication is minimal or nonexistent and the trust is absent.

If you find yourself in this situation, there are tools to help you maintain workplace relationships when they are strained. One suggestion that we discussed in chapter 7 is the importance of maintaining good boundaries. Something I recommend to clients and will now share with you—when dealing with strained workplace relationships, remember you are there to do a job, not make friends. Focus on doing your job and doing it well, because that is what you are hired to do.

Clients have found this helpful when the conflicts involved those who were also work "friends." This type of conflict can be a slippery slope because we tend to want to make the friendship the primary relationship at work, especially if there is an issue; however, at work, your primary relationship and priority is what you are being paid to do. Focusing on your job is also advised if the conflict is not with a friend, because it will be harder for an employer to justify disciplinary action because of interpersonal conflict over, say, poor work performance. And finally, the communication strategies for interpersonal conflict discussed in chapter 9 can also be helpful in maintaining strained workplace relationships. It is generally a good idea when communicating with others (whether there is conflict or not) to speak without being offensive and listen without being defensive and to seek clarity and understanding often. Because the truth is, we don't have to like the people we work with (and vice versa)—this ain't high school where we all need to be friends—but we do need to respect one another and do the job that we all are being paid to do. Period.

MAKING THE DECISION

If you've ever had to make work *work*, then you know how difficult staying in that environment can be. But deciding to walk away is not necessarily a walk in the park, either, because family and financial obligations and fear aren't the only reasons we struggle with knowing whether to stay in or leave a job. Sometimes, our struggle is due to a lack of decision-making skills. I see this with many of my clients in private practice. They sometimes struggle with making decisions confidently, which causes them to get overwhelmed and ultimately make no decisions. What we don't realize in those moments is that no decision is still a decision. By not making a decision, you have decided to continue on with a situation that is not working for you. Fortunately, decision-making is a skill you can learn and become proficient in.

As we've discussed, the decision to stay at or leave a workplace can have a range of personal and professional implications. However, there is a payoff in making confident decisions about your future at a job. In the first place, doing so will help you to feel in control. I've had clients who decided to stay in their job even though there were ongoing challenges at work. The decision to stay forced some of them to think of creative and alternative ways to navigate work, which made them feel in control. In other words, they made work work for them.

Further, when we feel in control of our decisions, we feel self-empowered. I am sure you can recall how good you felt when you made an important decision for yourself—more so if that decision paid off! Because we as Black women are often on the receiving end of other people's poor decisions at work, those experiences can cause us to feel helpless. Therefore, effective decision-making is a helpful skill that promotes self-care and self-empowerment.

BUILDING DECISION-MAKING SKILLS

In this exercise, we'll practice a protocol to help you make decisions with confidence.

The first step is to **identify the decision to be made**. While the focus of this chapter is about whether to stay in or leave a job, identifying the decision you need to make is the place to start with any decision in any area of life because it helps you to anchor your thoughts. When we are overwhelmed with work or a decision, we experience a lot of mental clutter that makes it hard to focus and concentrate. Taking a moment to step back and ask yourself, "What is the decision I need to make right now?" can help you start the process of making the right decision in the end.

To help guide the process, **develop a pros and cons list**. This is a tried-and-true tool I continue to teach my clients in order to promote healthy decision-making. The benefit of developing a pros and cons list is to help you to take the decision out of your head, making it easier to evaluate. Additionally, there's some real catharsis in the act of making the list—it's why journaling and writing are so therapeutic. They allow us to release our thoughts and feelings onto a material space to free up our mental space.

The process is simple, and you've probably done it before; if not on paper, then just by working it out in your mind. Create columns, one for pros and one for cons. Write the decision at the top of the page to help you stay focused. Starting with the pros column, ask yourself, "How would this decision help me or the situation?" Next, write down *all* of the benefits you can think of in the pros column. It is important to not judge the pros that you identify even if you think they are negative or "not a good reason" (e.g., "It's a job"; "I make good money and have benefits"; "I get discounts on stuff"). Follow the same process to create your cons list, but this time ask yourself, "How would this decision hurt me or the situation?" Write down *all* of the cons in that column (e.g., "I will lose my benefits"; "Having to find another job that pays the same or better"; "I will lose my discounts"). Again, try not to judge the cons you identify. Be honest with yourself about the pros and cons of the decision because, ultimately, you're the one most affected by what you decide. The goal is to be able to evaluate your list and make a decision based on what will benefit you the most.

Once you have created your pros and cons list, it's time to **evaluate your pros and cons list** to clarify the merits of your decision. What do you notice about the list? A list with more pros than cons is indicative of a decision that is likely to be more beneficial to you than not. Conversely, a list with more cons than pros should give you pause, because the decision could hurt you more than it helps. It is important to note that quantity alone may not be a definitive factor in evaluating the pros and cons list. For example, a pros and cons list to decide whether to leave your job might show two pros (e.g., peace of mind, more balance) and four cons (e.g., having to find another job, losing benefits, investment of time lost, loss of relationships), but you might decide that having peace of mind and more balance outweighs any of the cons on your list. Decision-making is not a perfect science. Developing and evaluating a pros and cons list helps you make a more informed decision, not a perfect one. In evaluating your list, you are looking for whether your reasons justify your decision and whether they suggest the need to consider an alternative decision (e.g., stay in your job). If the latter occurs, repeat the steps until you feel comfortable with your decision. There is no magic number here.

Finally, you will **implement the decision and reassess as necessary**. Once you have evaluated the pros and cons list, make the decision that *you* can justify and live with. This is important to remember because not everyone will agree with your decision, and they may give you a thousand reasons why you should do something different. Navigating conversations about your decision can be tricky, particularly if you are not rooted in the justification for your decision, so starting there is critical to any conversations with others. But when the moment arises for you to share your decision, consider asking yourself, "What is the most important thing that ____ needs to know about my decision (e.g., decision to leave job due to health reasons, decision to stay in job due to financial reasons) and what is the best way (e.g., in person versus by phone) and time (e.g., as soon as possible versus after you've already left) to do that?" The point of going through the process outlined above is so that you can be anchored and confident in whatever you decide. However, it is a good practice to assess later whether your decision had the anticipated benefits or consequences. There's always something we can learn from the decisions we make even if we learn that we made a bad one.

The decision to stay in or leave a job is never easy or perfectly clear. As Black women, we may make work decisions that can have ripple effects on those around us, which makes a hard decision even harder. But decision-making, like many of the things we've discussed throughout the book, is a skill that you can learn and gain proficiency in. The strategies in this chapter were intended to not only help you feel more confident in making a decision that centers you in your choice to stay in or leave a job but also help you minimize the guilt of centering yourself in your decision-making. Self-care is your primary job, and when you do that job well, you are able to show up more healthily and effectively at work and in life.

That's the new game—the one where we win when we are well!

HELPFUL TIPS

- Decision-making is a skill, not a science. Having a process to evaluate and make the right decision is important.
- The right decision may not be the most comfortable. Seek support as necessary.
- The right decision for you may not be best for others. Decide wisely.

Epilogue

IT'S OUR TIME!

Ecclesiastes 3:1–2 and 3:4 says, "For everything there is a season...a time to plant and *a time to harvest*...a time to cry and *a time to laugh*...a time to grieve and *a time to dance*." And if this book is any indication of the season for Black women, I would say that it's our time!

It's our time to reap the harvest of our labor! For so long we have been overlooked, overworked, and underpaid; shut down and shut out; invisible and ignored. The time has come for you to know your worth, show your worth, and demand to be paid your worth.

Affirmation: "I deserve the fruits of my labor."

It's our time to have joy! Experiences of shame, guilt, fear, and regret have robbed us of our right—our divine right—to live a life of joy, peace, and abundance. The time has come for you to live the life that you create for yourself.

Affirmation: "I will not live my life by any script other than the one I write."

It's our time to celebrate! Black women have carried the sorrows of the world on our shoulders and in our bodies—and we are tired of being sick *and* tired! Suffering is optional. The time has come for you to live a life of excitement and enthusiasm because you *believe* that you deserve it.

Affirmation: "I deserve to have joy!"

The time is now for you to live a life that is well, whole, and free. My hope for you is that *Playing a New Game* will be a tool that will continually inspire and ignite you to live and thrive unapologetically—because when you are well, I am well, and when we are well, we are stronger together. Now—go forth in boldness, in wellness, and in happiness. IT'S THRIVING TIME!

ACKNOWLEDGMENTS

So many hands, hearts, and minds went into my journey to make *Playing a New Game* possible.

First, I thank God for being my compass and companion on this journey. There were times when I wasn't sure if I could or should write this book, but your light guided me through the detours, distractions, and difficulties. I pray that this book brings you honor and blesses all who read it.

To Juan, my husband, my best friend, my rock, and my answered prayer—thank you, thank you, thank you! Thank you for loving and supporting me through this process. Thank you for seeing in me what I haven't always been able to see in myself. Thank you for encouraging me when I felt discouraged and helping me put the pieces together when I was falling apart. Thank you for taking such good care of our boys and their mama. I love you always!

To my sons, Deven, Ellison, and Quontavious, I love you and am proud of you. Thank you for giving your mama the space to write this book and inspiring me to be a better woman, mother, and human. I strive to leave you a legacy that you can be proud of and build on. My love for you is boundless.

To my mama, thank you! Our relationship has not been perfect. At times I had to search for your love in the hardness, but I never doubted the love was there. The sacrifice. The struggle. The striving. I get it now. In learning and understanding your story, I have been able to unpack, understand, and unapologetically tell my own and, in doing so, create spaces for others to tell and honor their stories. Thank you for your love, support, and encouragement in writing this book. I hope you are proud. I love you!

Thank you to my sisters, Annette, Ashley, Bobbie, Shannon, and Val (rest in peace). I love you and am proud to be your sister. Thank you for your love and prayers along this journey.

Many thanks to my aunts and uncles, nieces and nephews, cousins, in-laws, and ancestors for their love, prayers, and support. I pray that y'all are proud.

To my day ones and day twos, thank you for your friendship, love, and support. I am blessed with friends who've never doubted for a second that I would write this book and put it out into the world. I love you!

To my mentors who have guided me along the way, thank you! Dr. Sandra Richardson Williams, thank you for being not only my mentor but also my second mama and friend. Your wisdom and faith have blessed me more than you know. Dr. Sejal Parikh Foxx, I was so excited the day I walked into the doctoral internship class and saw that a woman of color was the instructor. You gave me a glimpse of what it might look like for me as a Black female counselor educator. More importantly, I am grateful to you, as my dissertation chair, for your careful guidance and direction of my research, which forms the basis of this book. From the very beginning, you believed in me and my research and ensured that I completed a dissertation that I could be proud of. Sorry that I never finished the article we were supposed to write—hopefully this book makes up for it! To Dr. Lyndon Abrams—you are a master teacher. You are a gift. You are a gentle soul. Words cannot describe how much I appreciate your mentorship and support. Thank you! Thank you also to Valerie M. Grubb for your mentorship at the Women's Leadership Academy. Your support and accountability were instrumental in pushing me to find the literary agent that I prayed for.

Thank you to Ginger, Faith, Felicia, Jasmine, Keisha, Libby Lou, Lisa, Olivia, Stacey, Tomeka, Trish, and Yellow-Bone—the twelve participants whose voices contributed to my doctoral research and the development of this book. I am forever grateful to these women for sharing their stories to offer a deeper understanding of Black women's experiences of race and gender stereotypes at work and provide a framework for other Black women to navigate those experiences.

Thank you to the countless women who have connected with me after speaking events to thank me for writing a book that speaks to their experiences at work. Those connections reminded me of the importance and urgency of bringing this book to the world.

Thank you to Elizabeth "Liz" Broekman and Fidelity Bank P.O.W.E.R. for sponsoring and supporting my work to help women live, love, and lead. Liz, I am forever grateful for you!

Thank you to Loyola University New Orleans's Women's Leadership Academy for your support and for being a safe container during the pandemic for me to grapple and grow into the confidence I needed to write and speak the words of truth that people need to hear.

Dr. Shannon Madden, thank you! I am grateful to you for your insightful and thoughtful editing and proofreading of the manuscript. Thank you for helping me to make this book better.

Thank you to my editor, Nana K. Twumasi, for believing in this project. I feel so blessed to work with you and am forever grateful for your support and commitment to bringing this book to market. A huge thank-you also to the whole Balance team for helping to bring this book to life and get it into the hands of readers.

Last but certainly not least, I want to thank my literary agent, Keely Boeving. I prayed for an agent who was not only passionate about finding the right publisher for this book but also someone that I could trust to honor and respect my voice and my work. God sent me you.

NOTES

Introduction

1. "Leading Causes of Death—Females—Non-Hispanic Black—United States, 2016," Women's Health, Centers for Disease Control and Prevention (CDC), last reviewed September 17, 2019, https://www.cdc.gov/women/lcod/2016/nonhispanic-black/index.htm.

2. "Obesity and African Americans," US Department of Health and Human Services, Office of Minority Health, last modified March 26, 2020, https://minorityhealth.hhs.gov/omh/browse.aspx?lvl=4&lvlid=25.

3. Elizabeth A. Pascoe and Laura Smart Richman, "Perceived Discrimination and Health: A Meta-analytic Review," *Psychological Bulletin* 135, no. 4 (July 2009): 531–54, https://doi.org/10.1037/a0016059.

4. J. Camille Hall, Joyce E. Everett, and Johnnie Hamilton-Mason, "Black Women Talk About Workplace Stress and How They Cope," *Journal of Black Studies* 42, no. 2 (March 2012): 207–26, https://doi.org/10.1177/0021934711413272.

Chapter 2: "You're an Overachiever"

1. "Title VII of the Civil Rights Act of 1964," US Equal Employment Opportunity Commission, accessed December 20, 2021, https://www.eeoc.gov/statutes/title-vii-civil-rights-act-1964.

Chapter 3: Changing the Game: Wellness as the New Playbook for the Workplace

1. Tammy Lewis Wilborn, "A Phenomenological Study of Working Class Black Women's Lived Experiences with Race and Gender Stereotypes in

the Workplace" (PhD diss., University of North Carolina At Charlotte, 2015), p. 1.

2. Wilborn, "A Phenomenological Study," p. 19.

3. Wilborn, "A Phenomenological Study," p. 71.

4. Wilborn, "A Phenomenological Study," p. 23.

5. Robin Bleiweis, Jocelyn Frye, and Rose Khattar, "Women of Color and the Wage Gap," Center for American Progress, November 17, 2021, https://www.americanprogress.org/article/women-of-color-and-the-wage-gap/.

6. Wilborn, "A Phenomenological Study," p. 68.

7. Wilborn, "A Phenomenological Study," p. 69.

8. *The State of Black Women in Corporate America 2020*, Lean In, accessed December 20, 2021, https://leanin.org/research/state-of-black-women-in-corporate-america.

9. Wilborn, "A Phenomenological Study," p. 85.

10. Wilborn, "A Phenomenological Study," p. 86.

11. Jasmine A. Abrams, Ashley Hill, and Morgan Maxwell, "Underneath the Mask of the Strong Black Woman Schema: Disentangling Influences of Strength and Self-Silencing on Depressive Symptoms Among Black Women," *Sex Roles* 80, no. 9–10 (May 2019): 517–26, https://doi.org/10.1007/s11199-018-0956-y.

12. Brea L. Perry, Kathi L. H. Harp, and Carrie B. Oser, "Racial and Gender Discrimination in the Stress Process: Implications for African American Women's Health and Well-Being," *Sociological Perspectives* 56, no. 1 (Spring 2013): 25–48, https://doi.org/10.1525/sop.2012.56.1.25.

13. J. Camille Hall, Joyce E. Everett, and Johnnie Hamilton-Mason, "Black Women Talk About Workplace Stress and How They Cope," *Journal of Black Studies* 42, no. 2 (March 2012): 207–26, https://doi.org/10.1177/0021934711413272.

14. "Leading Causes of Death—Females—Non-Hispanic Black—United States, 2016," Women's Health, Centers for Disease Control and Prevention (CDC), last reviewed September 17, 2019, https://www.cdc.gov/women/lcod/2016/nonhispanic-black/index.htm.

15. Hall, Everett, and Hamilton-Mason, "Black Women Talk About Workplace Stress."

16. Jihan Thompson, "Why Are So Many Black Women Suffering Through Infertility in Silence?," *Women's Health*, October 29, 2018, https://www.womenshealthmag.com/health/a23320626/infertility-race-survey/.

Chapter 4: Take Care of the Basics

1. Paris B. Adkins-Jackson, Jocelyn Turner-Musa, and Charlene Chester, "The Path to Better Health for Black Women: Predicting Self-Care and Exploring Its Mediating Effects on Stress and Health," *Journal of Health Care Organization, Provision, and Financing* 56 (September 2019): 1–8, https://doi .org/10.1177/0046958019870968.

2. "Sleep by the Numbers," National Sleep Foundation, May 12, 2021, https:// www.thensf.org/sleep-facts-and-statistics/.

3. "Coping with Stress," Mental Health, CDC, last reviewed July 22, 2021, https://www.cdc.gov/mentalhealth/stress-coping/cope-with-stress/.

4. Jodi Clarke, "Foods to Help Fight Depression," Verywell Mind, last updated May 11, 2020, https://www.verywellmind.com/foods-for-depression-4156403.

5. Joe Leech, "7 Science-Based Health Benefits of Drinking Enough Water," Healthline, last updated June 30, 2020, https://www.healthline.com /nutrition/7-health-benefits-of-water.

6. Tammy Lewis Wilborn, "A Phenomenological Study of Working Class Black Women's Lived Experiences with Race and Gender Stereotypes in the Workplace" (PhD diss., University of North Carolina at Charlotte, 2015), 1–140.

7. J. Camille Hall, "It Is Tough Being a Black Woman: Intergenerational Stress and Coping," *Journal of Black Studies* 49, no. 5 (2018): 481–501, https://doi .org/10.1177/0021934718766817.

Chapter 5: Protect Your Peace

1. *2014 ACA Code of Ethics*, American Counseling Association, 3, https://www .counseling.org/resources/aca-code-of-ethics.pdf.

2. "Types of Mental Health Professionals," National Alliance of Mental Illness (NAMI), updated April 2020, https://www.nami.org/About-Mental-Illness /Treatments/Types-of-Mental-Health-Professionals.

Chapter 8: Find Your People

1. Angela Neal-Barnett, Robert Stadulis, Marsheena Murray, Margaret Ralston Payne, Anisha Thomas, and Bernadette B. Salley, "Sister Circles as a Culturally Relevant Intervention for Anxious African American Women,"

Clinical Psychology: Science and Practice 18, no. 3 (September 2011): 266–73, https://doi.org/10.1111/j.1468-2850.2011.01258.x.

2. Quenette L. Walton and Olubunmi Basirat Oyewuwo-Gassikia, "The Case for #BlackGirlMagic: Application of a Strength-Based, Intersectional Practice Framework for Working with Black Women with Depression," *Affilia: Journal of Women and Social Work* 32, no. 4 (November 2017): 461–75, https://doi.org/10.1177/0886109917712213.

3. J. Camille Hall, "It Is Tough Being a Black Woman: Intergenerational Stress and Coping," *Journal of Black Studies* 49, no. 5 (2018): 481–501, https://doi.org/10.1177/0021934718766817.

4. Hall, "It Is Tough Being a Black Woman."

5. Eileen Linnabery, Alice F. Stuhlmacher, and Annette Towler, "From Whence Cometh Their Strength: Social Support, Coping, and Well-Being of Black Women Professionals," *Cultural Diversity and Ethnic Minority Psychology* 20, no. 4, (2014): 541–49, https://doi.org/10.1037/a0037873.

6. Aisha M. B. Holder, Margo A. Jackson, and Joseph G. Ponterotto, "Racial Microaggression Experiences and Coping Strategies of Black Women in Corporate Leadership," *Qualitative Psychology* 2, no. 2 (2015): 164–80, https://doi.org/10.1037/qup0000024.

7. Tammy Lewis Wilborn, "A Phenomenological Study of Working Class Black Women's Lived Experiences with Race and Gender Stereotypes in the Workplace" (PhD diss., University of North Carolina at Charlotte, 2015), 1–140.

8. Jasmine A. Abrams, Ashley Hill, and Morgan Maxwell, "Underneath the Mask of the Strong Black Woman Schema: Disentangling Influences of Strength and Self-Silencing on Depressive Symptoms Among Black Women," *Sex Roles* 80, no. 9–10 (May 2019): 517–26, https://doi.org/10.1007/s11199-018-0956-y.

9. Cheryl L. Woods Giscombé, "Superwoman Schema: African American Women's Views on Stress, Strength, and Health," *Qualitative Health Research* 20, no. 5 (2010): 668–683, https://dx.doi.org/10.1177%2F1049732310361892.

Chapter 9: Battle Wisely

1. Jioni A. Lewis, Ruby Mendenhall, Stacy A. Harwood, and Margaret Browne Huntt, "Coping with Gendered Racial Microaggressions Among Black

Women College Students," in "Black Girls' and Women's Resistance Strategies," special issue, *Journal of African American Studies* 17, no.1 (March 2013): 51–73.

2. Tammy Lewis Wilborn, "A Phenomenological Study of Working Class Black Women's Lived Experiences with Race and Gender Stereotypes in the Workplace" (PhD diss., University of North Carolina at Charlotte, 2015), 1–140.

3. Dove and the CROWN Coalition, *The CROWN Research Study: Creating a Respectful and Open Workplace for Natural Hair* (Unilever: 2019), 4, https://static1.squarespace.com/static/5edc69fd622c36173f56651f/t /5edeaa2fe5ddef345e087361/1591650865168/Dove_research_brochure2020 _FINAL3.pdf.

4. Wilborn, "A Phenomenological Study," p. 74.

5. "About," CROWN Act, accessed December 19, 2021, https://www.thecrownact .com/about.

INDEX

ABOUT THE AUTHOR

Dr. Tammy Lewis Wilborn is a retired board-certified licensed professional counselor-supervisor and former visiting assistant professor of counseling at the University of New Orleans. She is the owner of Wilborn Clinical Services, LLC, and Dr. Tammy Lewis Wilborn, LLC, and founder of the annual Black Women's Wellness Conference of New Orleans. Dr. Wilborn holds a PhD in counselor education and supervision from the University of North Carolina at Charlotte, an MS in counseling, and a BA in psychology from Loyola University of New Orleans. She lives in New Orleans, Louisiana, with her husband and two sons.